Tapestries
and their
Mythology

Endpapers:
Front The Story of Hercules (8th Labour)
Back   Paris being defended by Aphrodite at the
         Battle of Troy

Frontispiece: A 15th Century Arras Tapestry fragment

Tapestries and their Mythology

Jack Franses

John Gifford, London
1973

To my wife Philippa

© 1973 Jack Franses

First published 1973 by
John Gifford Ltd
125 Charing Cross Road
London WC2H 0EB

ISBN   0 7071 0463 7

Printed in Great Britain by
The Hope Burgess Group
London and Abingdon
Bound by
James Burn Ltd., Esher

Contents

Contents

List of Plates (Black and White)

(Colour)

Preface

As a young man I had access to a large library of books about tapestry, and found myself very frustrated with the thousands of plates which described the mythological subjects so briefly. In fact, only the names of the characters, and no story or explanation, were given. This made each plate a challenge.

Therefore, my sole aim in writing this book is to assist you, and me, in what I at first thought an impossible task. That is, somehow to find a simple way to identify mythological subjects in tapestries or paintings, for the artist was inspired by the endless events in mythology.

The method I have used is first, to simplify the mythology by making each story as brief as possible, cutting out the dead wood; then to provide a symbols index and a main index, which will enable you quickly to find not only the subject, but also a simplified version of the original story. I have included chapters on: Tapestries in general; Tapestry weaving; Tapestries as an investment; Philosophers; and finally, on artists who painted designs for tapestries.

Introduction

TAPESTRIES AND NEEDLEWORKS . . . WAS THIS THE BEGINNING?

According to Apollonius, the Babylonian women excelled in making decorative hangings. The temples of their gods, the palaces of their kings, were furnished with storied tapestries. The Assyrian Kings had sumptuous tapestries woven with gold and silver thread, which portrayed the Greek fables of the gods, The Iliad, The Odyssey, Andromeda, Arachne, Orpheus, etc. as well as their own traditions, such as Gilgamesh and Enkidu. The famous tapestries which, in the time of Metellus Scipio were sold for 800,000 sesterces (£8,000) and which were later bought by Nero for 2,000,000 sesterces (£20,000), were of Babylonian origin. For many ages the East retained the distinction of supplying Europe with stuffs, hangings and woven or embroidered tapestries.

These precious fabrics were wrought by the Greeks and Romans. Homer frequently makes mention of works of this kind; notably, while the Greeks were besieging Troy, Helen whiled away the hours by making embroideries depicting the combats of the heroes who were

Plate 1.   A section of the Bayeux Tapestry, circa 1066

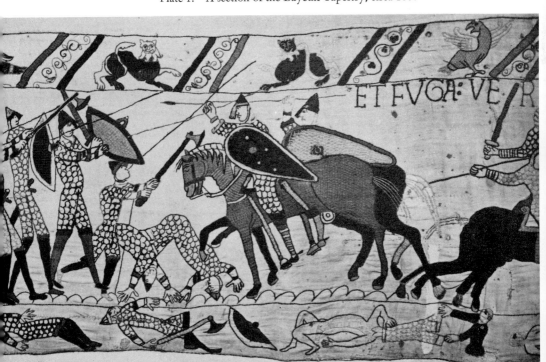

Plate 2. A fine Louis XV Beauvais Tapestry, cartoon by François Boucher, circa 1760. Size 10′ high × 9′ wide

slaying one another on her account. At the same time, back in Greece, Penelope was endlessly weaving the tapestry (web) portraying the exploits of her husband Odysseus. So Greek literature constantly reminds us of the roles played by pictorial fabrics in courtly affairs.

A.D. 830 In an Auxerre Church many fabric hangings were made for the St. Anthelme Bishop.

A.D. 985 The manufacturing of tapestries and of various stuffs was established in the Monastery of St. Florent de Saumur.

A.D. 1025   In the eleventh century 'England was inferior to none in point of skill and taste' said Dudon of the 'Chronique des Ducs de Normandie' referring to a specimen of magnificent embroidery designated as English work. The same chronicle tells us that the Duchess Gonnor, wife of Richard I, with the aid of her embroideresses prepared hangings of linen and silk depicting the Virgin and the Saints to embellish Notre Dame de Rouen. The Bayeux Tapestry attributed to Queen Matilda, wife of William the Conqueror, is the oldest work of its kind in existence (1066). (*Plate* 1)

It was in the twelfth century, after the return from the Crusades, that the West cultivated a great desire for these wonderful tapestries. These depicted the pious legends of the Saints or the feats of warriors and covered the castle walls giving an impressive elegance which could not fail to fill the mind with inspiring visions and noble emotions. In the fifteenth and sixteenth centuries weaving centres were numerous and tapestries appeared in all their glory on the walls of castles, monasteries and churches. The early tapestry designs were usually of biblical subjects. Today most tapestries for sale are from the sixteenth century onwards and Gothic examples are rare. The majority of early works were very large, sixteen feet high and with lengths of twenty

Plate 3.   Late Gothic Tapestry depicting a Medieval romance, circa 1570. Size 11' high × 13' 6" wide

feet or more, and in their spacious settings would have appeared as small paintings do in contemporary homes. As the homes they were made for became smaller, so did the tapestries. Their colours were usually rich and magnificent.

As time passed, a steady flow of painters evoked endless subjects depicting historical, mythological, allegorical, armorial and important contemporary events. Later we find hunting and pastorals, and scenes of country life from works by such artists as David Teniers (the younger), 1610–1690; Jean-Antoine Watteau, 1684–1721; Francois Boucher, 1703–1770; and Jean-Honore Fragonard 1732–1806.

To learn this subject requires time and effort. Firstly one must have a keen eye, and be able to define the subject depicted on the hanging and to relate it to a particular event or artist. Secondly, one must be able to place it in its period. I hope to make this easier for you with the following examples placed in their periods:

Medieval before 1400
Gothic 1400–1510
Renaissance 1510–1600
Romantic and mythological 1600–1795
Modern and mixed 1795 to the present day

Plate 4.   A William Morris Tapestry (See page 21)

Tapestry Weaving

General

Three fragments of tapestry are exhibited in the Cairo Museum and on one of these appears the cartouche of Thotmosis III, which indicates that it was woven about 1440 B.C. There are, of course, many examples of weaving from Greek tombs from the third and fourth centuries before Christ, and then we have the Coptic textiles and tapestries from A.D. 100 to 800.

Tapestry weaving in Western Europe started in the eleventh or twelfth century, and by the end of the thirteenth century most of the weavers had formed corporations of guilds and were receiving from their reigning monarch a Charter of rules and privileges.

In the fourteenth century there were three great centres—ARRAS, PARIS and LONDON, the latter being the smallest. The largest, greatest and oldest was Arras, so much so that its name is still used today as a synonym for tapestries. In the last quarter of the thirteenth century, owing to a loss of wealth among the patrons, Arras workshops declined and some of the weavers moved to the nearby centres, but most of them were coaxed to Italy, where workshops were set up in FERRARA, FLORENCE, SIENA and many other small towns. During this period Germany possessed many weavers, but no large workshop ever evolved. As Arras declined small workshops in TOURNAI in France prospered, this town then became the leading centre of manufacturing, until the beginning of the sixteenth century when the weavers of the Royal Brussels workshops achieved the complete mastery, which they held for over a century. During the sixteenth century the Italian tapestries were much sought after, but were never as precious as those from Brussels.

During the seventeenth century tapestries were in great demand throughout Europe. Workshops were set up once again in England, France, Spain, Holland and Denmark. The most famous of these were in Aubusson, Gobelins (Paris) and Beauvais in France, and Mortlake in England. However, we must remember that the Royal Brussels workshops still produced excellent tapestries.

During the eighteenth century magnificent tapestries were produced throughout Europe. Peter the Great of Russia founded a workshop in St. Petersburg in 1716 and several small German workshops started up, but later in the same century two great centres closed. The first of these was in Florence in 1737 and the second in Brussels in 1794.

15

Plate 5.   A mid 17th Century Mortlake Tapestry depicting Hephaestus spreading
the net for Ares (See page 57)

16

Tapestry Weaving in England, Scotland and Ireland from the Thirteenth Century

In a parchment deed written in Latin, without date but within the reign of Henry III (1216–1272), there is mention of a John Walingforde (Tapicer). Whether he was a repairer of Tapestries or a weaver is not known. Later in the century a document dated 11th June 1274 gives a list of names which includes Ralph Le Tapiter and in 1282 the same name crops up again in another document with two other tapestry weavers, Walter Le Tapener and Adam Doget Le Tapener. We also find mention of Gerald Le Tapessyer in 1294. In 1344 King Edward III instituted an inquiry into the London manufacturing of tapestries but unfortunately the document is badly mutilated.

In 1392 the Earl of Arundel died, and in a document he bequeathed to his wife a set of tapestries which was lately made in London. *Sic,* the Blue Tapestries with red roses and armorials bearings—'*Le grand sale g'estoit d'arreynment fait à Londres del overaigne de tapeterye blew; ove roses rouges en ycell, et mes armes et les armes de mes fitz'*.

Scotland

EDINBURGH A.D. 1467–1486
The first worker of Arras was a John Dolace, who was employed in Edinburgh from 1467 to 1486, and received a regular annuity for his work under *royal patronage.*

England

A.D. 1561
The municipal authorities of Sandwich, Kent, sent 'The Secretary Cecil' a present of six Arras cushions, the first work of 'Flemish' weavers, who had emigrated because of religious persecution in A.D. 1561.

1565 THE SHELDON TAPESTRIES
Richard Hyckes established at *Barcheston* and *Weston* a tapestry plant under the patronage of, and financially backed by, an English country squire, *William Sheldon.* These works were later run by his brother Ralph Sheldon. One of the finest sets of Sheldon tapestries can be seen

at Hatfield House. They depict the Seasons, and all four tapestries bear the date 1611, and the coat of arms of Sir John Tracey (he was knighted by James I, appointed High Steward in 1609, and later became Viscount Tracy, 1642).

THE MORTLAKE TAPESTRIES A.D. 1611–1703

Sir Francis Crane started the Mortlake works under James I, and by 1619 the first tapestries were produced. In 1636 Sir Francis Crane died, and his brother took over the business. This brother, Captain Richard Crane, was not successful and sold the factory to King Charles I. The works were known as *The Royal Manufactory* or *King's Works* for tapestries. England was entering troubled times, and interest in tapestries waned although, contrary to popular impressions, the Roundheads made many attempts to revive the industry. During the reign of Charles II the work declined and in 1703 the workshops eventually closed. 1625 to 1635 was the golden era in the history of Mortlake. The designs were the best of the period, and included Raphael's Acts of the Apostles; the History of Vulcan and Venus; The Twelve Months; The

Plate 6. Early 18th Century Soho Tapestry depicting an Oriental scene. Size 10' high × 12' wide (See page 20)

Plate 7.   A Royal Windsor Tapestry depicting the Castle of Balmoral. The factory mark and date (1884) can be seen woven into the top right hand corner of the plain border. Size 9′ high × 5′ wide (See page 21)

Four Seasons; The History of Hero and Leander, by Francis Clein (Cleyn); Diana and Callisto; The Horses (Clein) etc. Rubens supplied the design for The Stories of Achilles (six tapestries), and Van Dyck not only designed borders for the Raphael cartoons, but also adapted portraits of Sir Francis Crane and himself for cartoon.

During the seventeenth century other tapestry works were opened at the following:

1670 Lambeth.

Lambeth was famous for 'The Horses' tapestries at the Victoria and Albert Museum, and the famous tapestries 'The Capture of Cassandra by Agamemnon after the Fall of Troy', in the possession of H.M. the Queen.

1685 Hatton Garden (Clerkenwell) Great Queen Street was famous for the Chinoiseries tapestries by John Vanderbank.

1685 Soho (moved to Poland Street 1760).

Soho was famous for its tapestry seat-covers at first, and later for finely designed tapestries by Paul Saunders.

In the eighteenth century three more tapestry works were founded.

1723 Chelsea set up by James Christopher le Blon, painter.

1750 Paddington founded by Peter Parisot, and later in the same year moved to Fulham.

1750 Fulham Parisot worked under the patronage of the Duke of Cumberland and had employed one hundred workers, but the success of this venture was short-lived and in 1755 the stock was put up for sale.

1755 Exeter The looms and tools of the Fulham works were purchased by Jean Ulric Passavant who removed them to Exeter, where the works long continued to flourish.

Ireland

1339 A Flemish colony of weavers was in existence in Kilkenny. They had taken up residence in an area now known as Flemming Town, then known as Flemish Town. In the sixteenth century, Kilkenny Castle was remodelled, and the 'Tapestry Chamber' was dismantled. The only information is that the suite consisted of six pieces, thirteen feet deep and varying from fourteen to twenty-two feet in length. The 'action' of pictorial drama is stated to be rather obscure Roman history.

1630 In the inventory of the Duke of Ormond there are thirty-two tapestries listed, which were mostly made on the Kilkenny looms which his Lady Margaret Fitzgerald had established for making tapestries, turkey carpets and linens. *1652* and *1675* These inventory lists show fifty tapestries at Caen, and at Dunmore and Clonmell fifty-one tapestries. Tapestry weaving continued in Ireland until 1824.

Nineteenth and Twentieth Century Tapestries

In the later part of the nineteenth century a committee, with its president Prince Leopold Duke of Albany, brought over from Aubusson many French weavers, with M. Henri as director. They set up an establishment in Old Windsor which produced a considerable number of tapestries, i.e. The Four Seasons; The Battle of Aylesford; A Tournament on London Bridge; Queen Elizabeth Opening the Royal Exchange; Queen Victoria Visiting Mansion House on the Occasion of her Jubilee in 1887; a set of Morte d'Arthur; four tapestries for Windsor Castle depicting views of the royal residences—Windsor Castle, Buckingham Palace, Balmoral Castle and Osborne House. Because of lack of support and patronage the works closed down.

However, in 1877 William Morris set up a tapestry loom and taught himself the art of weaving. A year later he taught a Mr. Dearle the art, and by 1881 they set up together a tapestry works in Merton Abbey. The first work was The Goose Girl, a panel designed by Walter Crane. Some verdures were produced which depicted the woodpecker and the forest. The foliage was designed by Morris and Dearle, and the animals, which included a lion and a fox, were designed by Philip Webb. The effect they sought to achieve was aesthetic and Pre-Raphaelite; they also entangled themselves in Jacobean textile designs. I believe the combination of these two influences has yet to find its full impact on the world of art, as it has up to now been under-rated.

The first showing of the works of this partnership was in 1888 at the Arts and Craft Exhibition. It was at this fair that Sir Edward Burne-Jones, as a friend, was asked to design all the figure work on the Morris tapestries. Many tapestries were woven depicting a wide range of subjects, i.e. The Building of the Temple; The Star of Bethlehem; The Seasons; *Angeli Laudantes*; The Primavera of Botticelli; The Quest for the Holy Grail; The Story of St. George; Verdures; Hunts.

After nineteen years of weaving and designing, William Morris died in 1896, and John Henry Dearle continued to run the works. In 1908 Dearle was praised for the high quality he produced. Weavers' names listed are: Martin, Taylor, Ellis, Berry and Glassbrook. Designers included Byam Shaw, Heywood Summer, Mrs. Adrian Stokes, and of course John Henry Dearle. The tapestry works continued until the early 1940s when the building was bombed.

In 1897 weavers who left the Royal Windsor tapestry works after its dissolution set up a workshop in Poland Street, Soho, under the guidance of Mr. Brignolles. The subjects portrayed were of Scottish origin, i.e. The History of the Clan MacIntosh, designs after Sacheverell-Coke; The Tragedy of Bog-na-Gicht; Lady MacIntosh raising the Clan for Prince Charles Edward, etc.

In 1912 the Marquis of Bute established a tapestry works in Edinburgh, and used two of the William Morris weavers, Berry and Glassbrook. They, with four other weavers, started their first set of tapestries, Lord of the Hunt, which was to be a pure Highland set. However, at the outbreak of war in 1914, all six weavers went to the front, and all six died in battle, never to see their work finished. By 1924 the set was completed by apprentices. The workshop is still open today and producing fine work. *Lord of the Hunt* (*Plate* 9)

Plate 8. 'The Pilgrim in the Garden'. Designed Sir Edward Burne-Jones woven in 1901 by weavers Taylor, Martin and Ellis. Note the Mer Abbey monogram. Size 5' 1" high × 6' 7" w (See page 21)

Plate 9. 'Lord of the Hunt'.
The first Tapestry woven in Edinburgh works 'Dovecot'. Size 13' 7" high × 31' wide (See page

Tapestry Weaving in America

The late William Baumgarten founded the first tapestry works in America at Williamsbridge in New York City. In 1893 he brought over from France a M. Foussadier, former master workman of the Royal Tapestry works in England. He brought with him a small loom and this was at once set up at 321 Fifth Avenue. The first piece of tapestry made was for a chair seat, and took about two weeks to produce. This was kept by William Baumgarten as a family heirloom. The second piece produced is now in the Field Museum in Chicago.

Four weavers soon followed M. Foussadier and in a few months more looms were built. By this time 321 Fifth Avenue had become too small and so William Baumgarten decided to find new premises. His choice fell on the little French district of Williamsbridge, where a restaurant and hotel were up for sale. This was conveniently situated on the Bronx river which at that time possessed excellent qualities for dyeing purposes. M. Foussadier was also a master dyer.

The next step for William Baumgarten was to secure apprentices with the view to using native labour and so become independent of foreign workers. He therefore offered boys a contract of two dollars per week for one year, four dollars per week for the second year, six for the third, and eight dollars per week for the fourth year. This proved very successful, and in the first year they produced a number of specimens such as curtains, portières, borders, and chair covers.

In 1894 the National Society of Sculpture of New York paid tribute to the Baumgarten tapestry works. Shortly after this William Baumgarten was asked to lecture before the Society of Sculptors taking with him samples of his work. He proved himself and his deep devotion to tapestries. His ambition was to make America a world centre for tapestries.

In May 1894, William Baumgarten arranged an exhibition of tapestries. Amongst the visitors was a Mr. P. A. B. Widener, who said that if Baumgarten would go to Philadelphia the following week, he would show him a room for which tapestries were required. The result was that, after submitting sketches of thirteen panels of pastoral scenes after Francois Boucher, plus two pairs of portières and furniture covering, Baumgarten secured the order for twenty thousand dollars. After fifteen months the order was completed and delivered.

This order was a blessing for William Baumgarten as it gave him the encouragement he most certainly deserved. By 1904 he had made

Plate 10. An American Tapestry depicting a scene by Joseph Vernet.
Size 8' high × 11' wide (See page 24)

the Williamsbridge works one of the most important in the world for quality against quality, design against design, competing with Gobelins, Beauvais and Aubusson. In the St. Louis exposition of 1904, William Baumgarten won the Grand Prize for two panels exhibited. Commissions soon followed from a large proportion of the leading American families. The factory closed in 1912.

In 1908 Albert Herter, a painter by profession, became so interested in texture that he set up in competition to William Baumgarten an establishment on East 33rd Street in New York. As time passed Albert Herter became a follower of William Morris of England as he liked the Gothic style for its coarseness and simplicity. He made a tapestry for Mr. E. H. Harman at Arden, a tapestry which was fifty feet long, five feet high and designed in the Gothic style. In 1912 he wove a set of twenty-six panels depicting the story of New York.

25

Tapestry Weaving Today

Today we are surrounded by concrete, steel and glass. These all ask for warmth, and this is where tapestries can play a most important part, not only in bringing together in a room many colours and shades, but also to give it atmosphere, as in medieval days when cathedrals, churches, and castles were adorned with tapestries.

We are fortunate to be able to call upon forty-six workshops on the Continent, and one main workshop in Edinburgh, all of which are prepared to weave tapestries to the customer's personal design. Although there is only one main workshop in Scotland, nevertheless there is an association of weavers throughout Scotland who are capable of weaving fine tapestries to order. In Aubusson there is still a school which teaches youngsters the art of tapestry weaving.

Let us first consider the designers of tapestries, and their backgrounds.

Plate 11. Archie Brennan's decorative country map. Cotton warp, wool and linen weft. Gobelin technique. Size 5′ 6″ high × 8′ 6″ wide

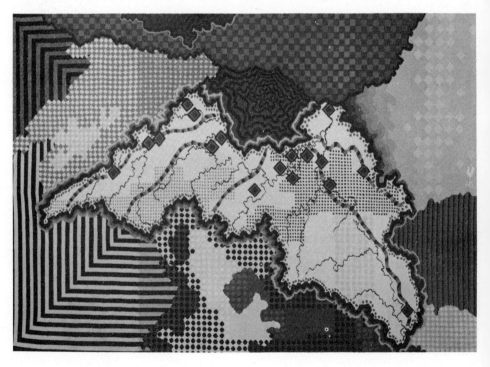

26

Plate 12. Woven in Edinburgh by Archie Brennan of the Dovecot works for St. Cuthbert's R.C. Church, Edinburgh. Cotton warp, woollen weft. Gobelin technique. Two panels size 14′ high × 3′ 3″ wide, 1971

Plate 14.   John Piper

Plate 13. Eduardo Paolozzi's 'The Whitworth Tapestry'. Cotton warp, woollen/linen
weft. Gobelin technique. Size 7′ high × 14′ wide

Tapestries Today

John Piper, painter and writer. His great love of beautiful buildings, especially churches, led eventually to tapestries, and he designed the tapestry for Chichester Cathedral (*Plate* 15 *and Plate* 15 *Colour*). John Piper also designed the Civic Hall tapestries at Newcastle, and has just finished a fine set for the Grocers' Hall (*Plate* 16 *Colour*). He is at present involved with the designing of yet another set of tapestries. These designs cover a varied range of subjects, but all give forth the strength and warmth and fine sensitivity of their designer.

Graham Sutherland, painter and designer. Between 1951 and 1958 he designed the tapestry for Coventry Cathedral. It depicts Christ in Majesty and measures seventy-four feet eight inches in height and thirty-eight feet in width (*Plate* 14 *Colour*).

	workshops		workshops
Austria	2	Norway	2
Belgium	2	Poland	6
Canada	2	Portugal	1
Czechoslovakia	2	Scotland	1
Denmark	1	South America	2
France	18	Spain	2
Germany	2	Sweden	1
Italy	3	U.S.A.	1
Jugoslavia	3		

There are also many artists who design and weave tapestries as a hobby.

Plate 15. A section from a Tapestry in Chichester Cathedral by John Piper
(See page 29)

Plate 16. A section from a Tapestry by Salvador Dali

Tapestries and Needleworks as an Investment

It is surprising how few people consider tapestries and needleworks as an investment. The main reasons are their lack of knowledge and certain misconceptions.

The following comments and replies might help clear up some of the common prejudices against tapestries and needleworks.

1. They are usually seen in museums and stately homes and these are invariably very large.

Small tapestries and needleworks are numerous.

2. They are overpowering.

The Verdure (depicting scenery and wildlife) which give a three-dimensional effect, are exactly the opposite.

3. They are covered with large figures which are sometimes far from handsome.

The later tapestries and needleworks usually have small graceful figures upon them.

Plate 17.   A late 16th Century Tapestry, 'Flemish Verdure'. Size 10′ high × 14′ wide

Aphrodite at her toilet

Plate 2. The Lady and the Unicorn

Plate 3. The Lady and the Unicorn

Plate 18.   A section from one of a set of four Tapestries depicting the four seasons 'Winter' designed by Louis Van Schoon, woven in Brussels in the late 17th Century. Size 12′ high × 17′ wide

Plate 19.   Aubusson Louis XV Tapestry depicting a Pastoral scene after J. B. Huet.
Size 8′ high × 13′ wide

Plate 20.   A fine 18th Century Beauvais Tapestry depicting a Grotesque.
Size 11′ high × 18′ wide

4. They depict religious subjects which are not always desirable.
There is a large selection of Genre subjects always available (i.e. country life and homely scenes).

5. They are old fashioned.
Can a love scene or a panorama (verdure) be old fashioned?

LIFE EXPECTANCY

Most tapestries and needleworks we find today were woven between the sixteenth and nineteenth centuries, and have survived with very little care and attention, although with central heating they dry out and tend to become brittle. A monthly vacuum cleaning and a wet cleaning every five to ten years by an expert will keep them fresh. Therefore I would give the life expectancy of one of these tapestries as being from six to nine hundred years or more. As there are many fourteenth and fifteenth century tapestries to be seen today I consider this a conservative estimate.

A DIFFERENT ROOM

Many modern homes which one sees are boring and conventional, although we all strive to produce an originality which nevertheless gives an atmosphere of beauty and tranquillity. Tapestries and needleworks have just these qualities, and can give a primitive or majestic look with warmth and power; they can transform the character of a room, and one can be made to feel in a different world by each tapestry, the choice of which seems to express the owner's individuality.

THE CHOICE

When choosing a tapestry or needlework the most important thing is that it should be pleasing to the eye of the purchaser. If one wishes to live with these tapestries and needleworks, then no matter how finely made, or how long a history they have, they must possess an attractive appearance. Exceptions can be made by the collector who wants examples of each type irrespective of colour or design. The main point is to be selective with knowledge behind you.

THE INVESTMENT

I have made a list of types of tapestries and needleworks, and placed them on charts showing the increase in value over the last two decades. These will give you a complete picture of the worth of tapestries as an investment. The charts below give exceptional sizes to show the extremes. What has not been shown is an allowance for bad condition, such as those which have been reduced (fragments), borders which are missing etc., although very often these can be classified as 'poor'. Sizes larger than a length of 18 feet by 12 feet in height, tend to lose value as they are difficult to utilise.

Plate 21. 17th Century Armorial Tapestry woven in Brussels by Geraert Peemans

The Investment Charts

Type	Quality	Width	Drop	1951	1961	1971	1972
RELIGIOUS 'A'							
16th to 18th Century							
Large	Poor	11 ft.×	9 ft.	£100	£300	£600	£900
figures	Medium	11 ft.×	9 ft.	£200	£350	£700	£1,000
	Good	11 ft.×	9 ft.	£300	£450	£800	£1,200
	Exceptional	11 ft.×	9 ft.	£400	£550	£1,000	£2,000
	Good	18 ft.×	12 ft.	£450	£600	£1,200	£2,500
	Good	9 ft.×	9 ft.	£300	£450	£850	£850
	Rare and						
	exceptional	11 ft.×	9 ft.	£800	£1,250	£3,500	£5,000
RELIGIOUS 'B'							
16th to 18th Century							
Small	Poor	11 ft.×	9 ft.	£200	£400	£600	£900
figures	Medium	11 ft.×	9 ft.	£300	£500	£800	£1,100
	Good	11 ft.×	9 ft.	£400	£800	£1,200	£2,000
	Exceptional	11 ft.×	9 ft.	£600	£1,200	£3,000	£4,500
	Good	18 ft.×	12 ft.	£400	£800	£1,500	£3,000
	Good	9 ft.×	6 ft.	£600	£1,200	£3,000	£4,000
	Rare and						
	exceptional	11 ft.×	9 ft.	£1,000	£3,000	£12,000+	£18,000
RELIGIOUS 'C'							
Colour plate							
Early 16th	Good	11 ft.×	9 ft.	£2,000	£4,000	£16,000	£25,000
Century	Exceptional	11 ft.×	9 ft.	£3,000	£6,000	£24,000	£32,000
or before	Rare	11 ft.×	9 ft.	£5,000	£10,000	£40,000	£60,000
	Special Subjects:						
	Last Supper,						
	Flight from Egypt						
ARMORIAL							
16th to 18th Century (Plate 21)							
	Medium	10 ft.×	7 ft.	£200	£400	£900	£1,200
	Good	10 ft.×	7 ft.	£300	£500	£1,200	£2,000
	Exceptional	10 ft.×	7 ft.	£500	£800	£2,000	£3,000
	Rare and						
	exceptional	10 ft.×	7 ft.	£900	£1,200	£4,500	£6,500
BEAUVAIS 'WORK'							
17th to 18th Century (Plate 2)							
Francois	Good	10 ft.×	10 ft.	£2,000	£6,000	£12,000	£16,000
Boucher	Exceptional	10 ft.×	10 ft.	£3,000	£9,000	£18,000	£25,000
CHINOISERIES							
18th Century (Plate 6)							
	Good	15 ft.×	9 ft.	£1,000	£2,500	£8,000+	£12,000
	Exceptional	15 ft.×	9 ft.	£2,000	£3,500	£12,000+	£20,000

Plate 22.   One of a set of 18th Century Aubusson Tapestries 'Drapes Rouges'
Size 9' high × 5' wide

Type	Quality	Width	Drop	1951	1961	1971	1972
CHOUX FLEUR							
16th to 18th Century (*Plate 71*)							
Feuille de	Medium	11 ft.×	9 ft.	£400	£1,200	£3,000	£6,000
Choux	Good	11 ft.×	9 ft.	£600	£1,800	£4,500	£9,000
	Exceptional	11 ft.×	9 ft.	£1,000	£3,000	£6,000	£12,000
	Good	18 ft.× 12 ft.		£1,000	£3,000	£6,000	£12,000
	Good	9 ft.×	6 ft.	£600	£2,000	£5,000	£10,000
	Rare and exceptional	11 ft.×	9 ft.	£1,500	£4,500	£15,000+	£30,000
CONTINENTS							
17th to 18th Century							
Set of 4							
tapestries	Good	15 ft.× 11 ft.		£4,000	£8,000	£20,000	£40,000
4 quarters							
of world	Exceptional	15 ft.× 11 ft.		£6,000	£12,000	£30,000	£60,000
FENETRE OR DRAPERIES ROUGES							
18th Century (*Plate 22*)							
	Poor	7 ft.× 10 ft.		£150	£250	£800	£1,200
	Medium	7 ft.× 10 ft.		£200	£350	£1,000	£2,000
	Good	7 ft.× 10 ft.		£400	£600	£2,000	£3,000
	Exceptional	7 ft.× 10 ft.		£600	£900	£3,000	£4,500
GOTHIC							
16th Century (*Plate 3 and Colour Plate*)							
	Medium	11 ft.×	9 ft.	£1,000	£4,000	£6,000	£12,000
	Good	11 ft.×	9 ft.	£1,500	£5,000	£8,500	£16,000
	Exceptional	11 ft.×	9 ft.	£2,000	£6,000	£15,000	£30,000
	Good	18 ft.× 12 ft.		£2,000	£6,000	£15,000	£30,000
	Good	9 ft.×	6 ft.	£1,500	£5,000	£8,500	£16,500
	Rare and exceptional	11 ft.×	9 ft.	£6,000	£15,000	£25,000	£50,000
GROTESQUE							
18th Century (*Plate 20*)							
	Good	10 ft.×	7 ft.	£1,000	£1,500	£6,000	£8,000
	Exceptional	10 ft.×	7 ft.	£1,500	£2,000	£8,000	£10,000
INDIES SERIES							
18th Century							
	Good	17 ft.× 13 ft.		£1,200	£2,000	£7,000	£10,000
	Exceptional	17 ft.× 13 ft.		£2,000	£3,000	£10,000	£13,000
MILLE FLEUR							
14th to 16th Century (*Plate 2*)							
	Medium	11 ft.×	9 ft.	£1,000	£3,000	£14,000+	£20,000
	Good	11 ft.×	9 ft.	£1,500	£5,000	£16,000+	£25,000
	Exceptional	11 ft.×	9 ft.	£2,000	£8,000	£45,000+	£60,000
MYTHOLOGICAL							
17th to 18th Century							
	Poor	11 ft.×	9 ft.	£150	£350	£1,000	£2,000
	Medium	11 ft.×	9 ft.	£250	£450	£1,500	£2,500
	Good	11 ft.×	9 ft.	£450	£650	£2,500	£4,000
	Exceptional	11 ft.×	9 ft.	£650	£850	£3,500	£5,000
	Good	18 ft.× 12 ft.		£450	£650	£2,500	£4,000
	Good	9 ft.×	6 ft.	£450	£650	£2,500	£4,000
	Rare and exceptional	11 ft.×	9 ft.	£1,000	£2,500	£5,000	£8,000

Type	Quality	Width	Drop	1951	1961	1971	1972

PASTORAL AND GENRE
17th to 18th Century (*Plate* 19)

Type	Quality	Width × Drop	1951	1961	1971	1972
	Poor	11 ft.× 9 ft.	£150	£450	£900	£1,200
	Medium	11 ft.× 9 ft.	£200	£800	£1,900	£2,500
	Good	11 ft.× 9 ft.	£300	£750	£2,500	£3,500
	Exceptional	11 ft.× 9 ft.	£450	£1,000	£3,500	£4,500
Extreme	Good	18 ft.×12 ft.	£400	£1,200	£3,000	£4,000
sizes	Good	9 ft.× 6 ft.	£200	£800	£2,000	£3,000
	Rare and exceptional	11 ft.× 9 ft.	£500	£1,500	£6,000	£8,000

DON QUIXOTE
17th to 18th Century

	Quality	Width × Drop	1951	1961	1971	1972
	Medium	11 ft.× 9 ft.	£500	£1,000	£4,000	£6,000
	Good	11 ft.× 9 ft.	£750	£1,500	£7,000	£9,000
	Exceptional	11 ft.× 9 ft.	£1,000	£3,000	£12,000	£15,000

SEASONS AND MONTHS
16th to 18th Century

Type	Quality	Width × Drop	1951	1961	1971	1972
Brussels	Medium	7 ft.×10 ft.	£200	£400	£1,000	£1,500
	Good	7 ft.×10 ft.	£300	£500	£1,500	£2,200
	Exceptional	7 ft.×10 ft.	£500	£800	£2,500	£3,500
Mortlake	Medium	7 ft.×10 ft.	£300	£500	£1,500	£2,200
	Good	7 ft.×10 ft.	£400	£600	£2,000	£3,000
	Exceptional	7 ft.×10 ft.	£600	£900	£3,000	£5,000

DAVID TENIERS SUBJECTS
17th to 18th Century (*Plates* 68, 69, 70)

	Quality	Width × Drop	1951	1961	1971	1972
	Medium	11 ft.× 9 ft.	£800	£1,200	£4,000	£8,000
	Good	11 ft.× 9 ft.	£1,200	£2,000	£6,000	£12,000
	Exceptional	11 ft.× 9 ft.	£1,600	£3,000	£10,000+	£16,000

VERDURE
16th to 18th Century (*Plate* 17)

Type	Quality	Width × Drop	1951	1961	1971	1972
Flemish	Poor	11 ft.× 9 ft.	£100	£350	£600	£1,200
	Medium	11 ft.× 9 ft.	£150	£450	£1,000	£1,500
	Good	11 ft.× 9 ft.	£200	£600	£2,000	£3,500
	Exceptional	11 ft.× 9 ft.	£350	£800	£2,500	£4,500
	Good	18 ft.×12 ft.	£350	£700	£1,200	£2,000
	Good	9 ft.× 6 ft.	£250	£700	£1,500	£2,500

VERDURE
16th to 18th Century

Type	Quality	Width × Drop	1951	1961	1971	1972
Brussels	Poor	11 ft.× 9 ft.	£150	£450	£1,000	£2,000
	Medium	11 ft.× 9 ft.	£200	£600	£2,000	£4,000
	Good	11 ft.× 9 ft.	£350	£800	£2,500	£5,000
	Exceptional	11 ft.× 9 ft.	£450	£900	£3,500	£6,000
	Good	18 ft.×12 ft.	£350	£800	£2,500	£5,000
	Good	9 ft.× 6 ft.	£200	£600	£1,800	£4,000

New Tapestries are woven from £400 per square foot.

40

Plate 23. An 18th Century Tapestry depicting one of the elements 'Water'.
Royal Gobelin. Size 11′ high × 9′ wide

41

Mythology

PERIODS IN DATE ORDER

1st. Prehistoric (Far East, Europe, Africa and America).
2nd. Egyptian: 4000 B.C. onwards.
3rd. Assyrio-Babylonian: 3000 B.C. onwards.
4th. Phoenician: 3000 B.C. onwards.
5th. Greek: 3000 B.C., reached its apex sixteenth century B.C.
6th. Indian: 3000 B.C.
7th. Persian: eighth century B.C.
8th. Modern China: sixth century B.C.
(Old China: see Prehistoric).
9th. Roman: third century B.C.
10th. Japanese: just pre-B.C.
11th. Celtic: just pre-B.C.
12th. Teutonic (German and Scandinavian): just pre-B.C.
13th. Slavonic: sixth century A.D.
14th. Finno-Ugric: sixth century A.D.

THE GODS AND GODDESSES

From the third century B.C. the Greek and Roman gods were equated and in addition the Greek gods were given new names:

GODS

Greek	*Roman*
Zeus	Jupiter
Poseidon	Neptune
Hephaestus	Vulcan
Hermes	Mercury
Ares	Mars
Apollo	Apollo

GODDESSES

Greek	*Roman*
Hera	Juno
Athene	Minerva
Artemis	Diana
Hestia	Vesta
Aphrodite	Venus
Demeter	Ceres

MINOR DIVINITIES

Greek	*Roman*
Selene	Luna
Eros	Cupid
Dionysus	Bacchus
Hades	Pluto

Plate 24. 'Banquet of the Gods'. 18th Century Royal Brussels Tapestry. Size 11' high × 18' wide

Plate 25.   Louise XIV French Tapestry depicting Acis, Galatea and Polyphemus.
Size 10′ 7″ high × 7′ wide (See page 45)

44

Mythology Characters

ACHILLES
Father: Peleus; mother: The Sea Goddess, Thetis.

Achilles was brought up by the Centaur Chiron, who fed him on marrow bones of bears and the entrails of lions. Thus he grew from strength to strength. When Achilles was nine the prophet Calchas predicted that he alone would conquer Troy; but his mother, who knew the boy would meet his death there, tried to avoid the peril by hiding him, disguised as a girl, in the Palace of Lycomedes, King of Skyros. Unfortunately the Greeks, helped by Odysseus, discovered the so-called 'maiden' by an ingenious trick. Odysseus one day came to the palace of Lycomedes with gifts for the King's daughters, among these gifts he slipped a shield and spear. Then he and his companions gave battle cries and sounded the trumpets. Achilles, thinking they were being attacked, rushed for the weapons. The Greeks then took him with them, for he could not escape his destiny.

We know he displayed valour beneath the walls of Ilium and in single combat he killed the valiant Hector. But he perished before Troy was taken, pierced in his vulnerable heel by an arrow, from the bow either of Paris or of Apollo.

ACIS, GALATEA AND POLYPHEMUS (*Plate* 25)
Acis and Galatea loved each other, but tragically the rival to Acis was the giant, Polyphemus, who paid his court to Galatea with a daily present of a bear or an elephant. The Cyclops Polyphemus decided to kill his rival, and one day he followed them to their hiding place in the hollow of a grotto. When Galatea left, Polyphemus crushed Acis under an enormous boulder. Galatea, however, succeeded in having Acis changed into a river by splitting open the boulder, and through the gash in the rock a tall, sturdy reed pushed upwards. The leaping waves of the Acis roared forth from the gash.

ACONTIUS AND CYDIPPE (*Plate* 26)
Acontius was a youth of the Island of Ceos. He went to Delos where he fell in love with Cydippe, whose parents forbade their marriage on account of his obscure origin. He wrote on an orange which he threw to Cydippe 'I swear by Artemis to marry no one but Cydippe'; and in return she did the same. When Cydippe's parents desired to marry her to other men. Cydippe fell ill. The parents consulted the oracle, and learned that the oaths were binding, so they permitted the marriage.

ACTAEON
Woe to the impudent man who gives way to his curiosity! Actaeon, son of Aristaeus and Autonoe was a passionate huntsman. One day,

Plate 26. A fine Antwerp Tapestry depicting Acontius and Cydippe, circa 1700
(See page 45)

with his hounds, he was chasing a stag when he came into the valley
of Gargaphia, near the fountain Pasthenius, where at that moment
Artemis and her companions happened to be bathing. Stunned by the
beauty of the goddess, Actaeon paused to contemplate her. He was
observed. Enraged that a mortal should have seen her in nakedness,
Artemis changed Actaeon into a stag and set his own pack on him.
The hounds tore Actaeon to pieces and devoured him.

ADONIS AND APHRODITE (VENUS) (*Plate* 27)
The mother of Adonis transformed herself into a tree, and from this
tree Adonis was born. He was of extraordinary beauty. At his birth
Aphrodite put him into a coffer which she gave into the care of the
Underworld goddess Persephone.

When, later, Aphrodite opened the coffer with Persephone, they
beheld such beauty that Persephone refused to give up the child.
Eventually the dispute was brought before Zeus (Jupiter) who decided
that Adonis should spend half the year on earth and half in the Underworld. Aphrodite fell deeply in love with Adonis and bore him a son
and a daughter. She feared a tragic fate would befall him, and tried to

46

Plate 27. A fine Mortlake Tapestry depicting the story of Adonis and Aphrodite, circa 1700
(See page 46)

47

discourage him from the chase. One day he was killed by a wild boar or bear. Where his blood soaked into the ground, up sprang the flower Anemone.

AENEAS

Son of Aphrodite (Venus) and the mortal Anchises.

Aeneas, the son-in-law of King Priam of Troy, was both intrepid and full of wisdom. He valiantly defended the City of Ilium in vain. His mother realised that all was lost and directed him to a waiting ship to which he carried his father, and with the few remaining Trojans escaped.

They went in search of a new place of settlement, and after trying to establish himself in Thrace, in Crete and in Sicily, he finally reached the banks of the Tiber. There he married the daughter of Latimus, and built a town called Lavinium.

Aeneas was venerated by the Romans, under the name of *Jupiter Indiges*, as the founder of their race; the great Roman families, notably that of the Julii, boasted that they were descended from him. He was made hero of the *Aeneid* by Virgil.

ALCMENE AND ZEUS

Zeus knew that Alcmene would produce a son who would one day be a powerful protector of both gods and men alike. In order to seduce Alcmene, Zeus had to use an unusual stratagem, for she was the wife of the Theban chief Amphitryon, and he knew she was virtuous and incorruptible. So he took advantage of Amphitryon's absence to assume Amphitryon's own appearance. Alcmene welcomed Zeus in this disguise exactly as though he were her actual husband. When the real Amphitryon returned a few hours later, he was surprised by his wife's lack of enthusiasm whilst she in turn was astonished that he had so quickly forgotten the marks of tenderness she had so recently bestowed upon him. The mystery was finally cleared up by the soothsayer Teiresias. From the double union twins were born— Hercules, son of Zeus, and Iphicles, son of Amphitryon.

APHRODITE (VENUS)

Daughter of Zeus and Dione.
Mother of Eros, Harmonia, and Hermaphroditus.
Goddess of Pure and Ideal Love in its noblest aspect as well as in its most degraded.

She protected marriages, and unmarried girls and widows prayed to her in order to get a husband. She was the Goddess of Lust and Venal Love, the patroness of prostitutes; also the Goddess of Fertility.

The Birth of Aphrodite

Cronus castrated his father, Uranus, and cast the severed genitals into the sea. They floated to the surface of the waters, producing a white foam, from which rose Aphrodite. She was carried across the sea to Cyprus and was greeted by the Horae, who conducted her to the Assembly of the Immortals. Hera and Athene were also very lovely, but the haughty beauty of Hera demanded respect, and the severe look of Athene arrested desire. Aphrodite exuded an aura of seduction. Paris was asked to choose the most beautiful and Eros offered a golden apple 'for the fairest'. This resulted in victory for Aphrodite. (See *Judgement of Paris*, p. 113). It was because she gave Helen, the wife of Menelaus, to Paris that the War of Troy started, and it did not cease until Helen returned to her husband.

Aphrodite's Magic Girdle

This could enslave the hearts of gods and men alike. It was a girdle, wondrously worked and cunningly embroidered, and contained every seduction of which Homer tells us—love, desire, and sweet dalliance— which can enthrall the heart of even the wisest. Aphrodite's beauty stirred all the gods, but it was Hephaestus, the ugliest and most graceless of all, who won her for his wife. Such an ill-matched union could not be happy, even on Olympus. Those who consoled her were Ares (see *Ares*, p. 57) and Hermes. Needless to say, Aphrodite took a delight in arousing the desires of all, and launching them on adventure. With the exception of Athene, Artemis and Hestia, all came under her influence.

The Power of Aphrodite

In Amathus, Cyprus, there lived a sculptor named Pygmalion, who shunned all women, and yet fervently venerated Aphrodite. One day he started work on a marble statue of a woman, which turned out to be of such extraordinary beauty that he fell in love with it. Aphrodite took pity on Pygmalion, and one day as he held the statue in his arms the marble suddenly moved and was miraculously alive.

APOLLO (*Plate* 28)

Father: Zeus; mother: Leto.

Apollo was first of all a God of the Light, a Sun-God without, however, being the Sun itself. As Solar God Apollo made the fruits to ripen, and at Delos and Delphi the first crops were therefore consecrated to him. In addition he protected the crops by destroying the mice which infested the fields (Apollo Smintheus), and also drove away locusts (Apollo Parnopius).

Because the Sun is murderous, with its rays which strike like darts, and at the same time beneficent because of its prophylactic powers,

Apollo was thought of as an Archer-God—as a God of Sudden Death; but also as a Healer God who drove away illness (Alexikakos). Apollo was also the God of Divination and Prophecy. His most celebrated sanctuary was at Delphi, situated in a deep cavern from which emanated prophetic vapours. The priestess, or pythia sat on a tripod place on the threshold of the cavern. When called upon to tell the future she fell into a trance under the god's influence and, possessed by prophetic delirium, began to pour forth broken phrases and obscure words which were then interpreted by the priest and members of the sacred counsel of Delphi.

Apollo was also a Shepherd-God (Nomius) whose mission it was to protect the flocks; a Wolf-God or else a god who killed wolves; a Ram-God who was also a pastoral divinity; a Musician-God and God of Song and Lyre, and a Colonising-God.

In spite of his multiple character, he was depicted as a young man of idealised beauty with a vigorous body, a broad chest and slim hips. He had a beardless face with delicate features, and is generally nude or wears only a chlamys thrown over his shoulder. When he is represented as a musician, he wears a long tunic with loose folds. His attributes are the bow, the quiver, the shepherd's crook, the lyre. The animals which are sacred to him are the swan, the vulture, the crow, the cock, the hawk, the cicada, the wolf and the serpent. His favourite plants are the laurel, the palm, the olive and the tamarisk.

Apollo's Exploits

Apollo's first exploit was with the serpent Python, which he killed with an arrow forged for him by Hephaestus. 'Torn with pain the monster lies shuddering: he rolls in the sand, he plunges into the forest and twists on the ground, until the moment when, with poisonous breath, he exhales his life in a torrent of blood'.[1] Apollo contemptuously pushed his victim aside and said 'Now rot where you lie'. And in memory of the occasion the spot was called *Pytho* (from the Greek 'to rot'). The name was later changed to Delphi. The memory of this event was perpetuated at Delphi every nine years by the festival of the Septeria (or Veneration). An adolescent youth was chosen from among the nobility to represent Apollo, and accompanied by other young folk he would set fire to a wooden hut which symbolised the dragon's lair.

Apollo slew the giant Tityus who had dared to assail the honour of Leto, his mother. He killed Phorbas, Chief of the Phlegyians, who used to lie in wait on the road to Delphi, and force passing pilgrims to fight with him. Having vanquished them he would then put them painfully to death. Apollo, disguised as an athlete, appeared one day and felled Phorbas with a mighty blow of his fist. Apollo even measured

[1] Larousse, *Mythology.*

his strength against Hercules, who seized the sacred tripod from Delphi and carried it away. Apollo hastened after him, overtook him and prepared to fight it out. Zeus put an end to the combat, obliged Hercules to restore the tripod and reconciled the two adversaries. Apollo, indeed, tolerated no insult to his person or cult. The archer Eurytus who dared to challenge him perished for his presumption, and because Agamemnon at Troy had offended his priest Chryses, for nine days Apollo let fly his exterminating arrows against the Greek army, sending innumerable warriors to Hades (the Underworld).

Apollo's Servitude

Apollo twice aroused the wrath of Zeus. The first time he was sent to Troy, where he served King Laomedon for a year. There he pastured the royal oxen on the slopes of Mount Ida, but when the year had run its course, the King refused to pay him. In revenge Apollo spread

Plate 28. The Chariot of Apollo (See page 49)   The Metropolitan Museum of Art

plague through the country. The second time Zeus sent him to serve Admetus, King of Pherae, and Apollo tended his mares and ewes. He showed devotion to his mortal master, helped him to get married, and even saved his life. Apollo watched his flock and played his lyre. Attracted by the divine music the fallow deer and hinds would come to frisk and even the savage beasts of the forest would join in. One day while strolling on Mount Tmolus, he was challenged to a musical contest by the Satyr Marsyas, who had acquired a remarkable virtuosity on the flute which Athene had once cast aside. A jury was constituted, among whom sat the Muses and Midas, King of Phrygia. When the tournament was finished Apollo was declared the victor. Only Midas voted for Marsyas. Apollo punished him by bestowing upon him a pair of ass's ears. As for his unfortunate rival, he attached him to a tree trunk, flayed him alive and suspended his body at the entrance of a cavern. It is sometimes said that the contest took place between Apollo and Pan.

The Loves of Apollo

It seemed that few females could resist him. Amongst those who could not were Oceanid, Clyte, Corycia, Acacallis, Cyrene, Psamathe, Coronos, Creusa, Deione and Thyria. Each had a child by him and some had two.

Three of these have special significance.

First Deione, who gave birth to Apollo's son Miletus, feared her father's (Mino's) wrath, and so had the baby carried into the forest where, thanks to Apollo's protection, the wolves took care of the newly-born child, who grew up among them. Later, shepherds discovered him and removed him from this savage existence.

The second was Thyria's son Cycnus, a youth of rare beauty who was attached to Phylius, his companion of the chase. When Phylius abandoned him, Cycnus in despair threw himself in Lake Canopus. Thyria, his mother, threw herself in after him; Apollo changed them both into swans.

The third, the nymph Cyrene, said to be the daughter of King Hypseus, was a huntress. Apollo saw her one day on the slopes of Mount Pelion wrestling with a lion. Charmed by her beauty and courage, he carried her away in a golden chariot to Libia, where she gave birth to Aristaeus.

Three Women who Refused Him (Plate 29)

The first was the nymph Daphne, who was as chaste as she was beautiful. When she refused to be ravished by him and fled, he overtook her and she already felt the eager arms of the god around her when she called upon the venerable Gaea to aid her. Immediately the earth gaped open, Daphne disappeared and in her place a laurel tree sprang

Plate 29. A fine Brussels Tapestry depicting the story of Apollo and Daphne, circa 1680 (See page 52)

from the ground. Apollo made it the plant sacred to him. (*Plate* 29)

The second was Castalia, a mortal girl from Delphi who threw herself into the fountain which afterwards took her name, in order to escape the god's pursuit.

The third, Cassandra, was the daughter of King Priam. Apollo conferred upon her the gift of foretelling the future on promise to yield herself to him. But Cassandra refused to fulfil her part of the bargain. Apollo begged a single kiss: in this way he breathed into her mouth, and though he left her with the power of foretelling the future, he took away her powers of persuasion so that from then onwards no one would believe what Cassandra predicted.

Several youths were also loved by Apollo. One such was Cyparissus, whom the god changed into a cypress because the young man was heartbroken at having killed a favourite stag. Then there was Hyacinthus, who was also loved by Boreas and Zephyrus: when Apollo and Hyacinthus were throwing the discus, Boreas and Zephyrus directed Apollo's discus so that it struck Hyacinthus on the head and immediately killed him. From the blood which gushed from the wound sprang the flower which bears his name, the Hyacinth. In memory of this sad event the people of Laconia annually celebrated the Festival of the Hyacinth, which began with funeral offerings and lamentations, and ended with songs of joy in honour of the young hero who had become immortal.

THE APPLES OF THE HESPERIDES' GARDEN

The apples of the Hesperides grew on a tree given by Hera (Juno) as a wedding gift when she married Zeus (Jupiter). They were guarded by the Hesperides (daughters of Atlas) and also by a many-headed dragon which never slept.

Hercules' eleventh labour was to obtain three golden apples from the garden of the Hesperides for his master Eurystheus, but only on the condition that he would return them. Otherwise the wrath of Hera would descend upon them. Hercules persuaded Atlas to ask his daughters to allow him to borrow three golden apples on the condition that they were returned. To do this, Atlas asked Hercules to hold up the world, whilst he fetched them. Hercules did this, but on Atlas's return, Atlas rejoiced in his new-found freedom and refused to give up the apples or to take on the great burden again of the heavens. However, Hercules tricked him by agreeing that Atlas could take the golden apples to Eurystheus, and asked Atlas if he could please hold up the heavens while he, Hercules, put a cushion on his shoulders, to ease the burden. Atlas fell into the trap and was once again left to hold up the heavens, although he threatened Hercules. Hercules never looked back and eventually returned the golden apples through Athene (Minerva).

Plate 30.   A fine Mortlake Tapestry depicting the nymphs dancing before the Apulian Shepherd appears circa 1700 (See page 57)

Plate 31.   Ares and Aphrodite (See page 57)   The Metropolitan Museum of Art Kennedy Fund

THE APULIAN SHEPHERD AND THE NYMPHS (*Plate* 30)
The nymphs lived in Pan's cave in Messapia, and played and danced in
the nearby woods. One day a passing shepherd from Apulia filled these
nymphs with sudden terror. However, when they recovered and
realised who was pursuing them, they returned to their dancing.
The shepherd mocked them, leaping clumsily about in imitation, and
hurling coarse insults and bad language. Nothing silenced him until a
tree trunk imprisoned his throat; his fingers sprouted twigs—and he
finally became a wild olive. In its bitter berries the tree reveals traces
of the Apulian shepherd's tongue and the harshness of his language.

ARACHNE
Arachne was famous for weaving tapestries and needlework. One day
she challenged Athena, the Goddess of Wisdom, Arts and Industry, to
see who could produce the best work. Disguised as an old woman,
Athena tried unsuccessfully to dissuade Arachne from her folly.
However, Arachne wove a great tapestry illustrating the disorderly
love affairs of the gods. Athena could find no fault with her work and
became very jealous, so much so that she turned Arachne into a spider
to weave forever the thread produced by her own body. The scientific
name for the spider family is *Arachnida*, and is derived from *Arachne*.

ARES (MARS) (*Plate* 31)
Son of Zeus and Hera.

Ares, God of War
By nature Ares was wicked and fickle. He enjoyed fights, and loved the
battlefield, striking deadly blows on both sides. His squires were
Deimos (Fear) and Phobos (Fright), Eris (Strife), Enyo (Destroyer of
Cities) and Keres (who eagerly drank the blood of the dying). Ares
was disliked for his perpetual thirst for blood, his brutality, and blind
violence, yet he rarely emerged victorious in combat.

When Ares challenged Hercules, who had just killed his son Cycnus,
Ares was wounded by the hero and was forced to return to Olympus.
When he fought Athene on the Plains of Ilium she beat him. He was
captured by two Aloadae and kept in a brass vase for thirteen months
and it was Hermes who enabled him to escape.

Ares' Loves (Plate 5)
Aphrodite fell in love with Ares and the sentiment was soon recipro-
cated. When Hephaestus, Aphrodite's husband, found out he forged a
net so fine that it could hardly be seen, and so strong that it could not
be broken. He arranged the net above the bed where they normally
frolicked, and pretended to leave for Lemnos. As soon as Hephaestus
departed Ares visited his home, and lay with Aphrodite. The couple

fell asleep and then the ingenious Hephaestus spread his net over them. Hephaestus then called to the gods 'Zeus and your immortals, come and see this intolerable thing, worthy of your laughter. I will not release them until you Zeus, return the gifts I made to you, for the hand of Aphrodite, who cannot restrain her lust.'

Then the gods gathered together and watched Ares and Aphrodite who were in a state of extreme confusion, which caused uncontrollable laughter from the gods. Ares promised to pay the price of adultery. Ares' favourite bird is the vulture, and his animal is the dog, as scavengers of the battlefield.

ARETHUSA AND ALPHEIUS

Arethusa was a wood nymph, daughter of Oceanus. She was very beautiful and liked hunting, and she was an attendant of Artemis. She was seen one day by Alpheius who immediately fell in love with her. He pursued her and, to escape him, at her request she was changed into a spring by Artemis. Alpheius, who remained in the neighbourhood of Olympia, changed himself into a river, and his waters crossed the sea without mingling with it, to join the waters of the spring Arethusa on the Isle of Ortygia.

Plate 32. A fine Gobelins Tapestry depicting Artemis resting after the chase, circa 1750 (See page 59)

ARTEMIS (DIANA) (*Plate* 32)
Other Roman names: Cynthia, Delia, Hecate, Lucina, and Phoebe.
Daughter of Zeus by Leto (Latona); the twin sister of Apollo.
Goddess of The Moon, of Hunting and also of Birth; as Lucina (Roman),
the Patroness of Unmarried Girls and of Chastity.

Her attributes were the Moon held in her hand, or the Moon and
stars which surrounded her head. She was clad in a short tunic which
did not fall below her knees, her feet were shod with cothurnus or
laced buskin, and she was usually accompanied by a hind or dog.
Very different is the crowned Artemis of Ephesus, whose body is
tightly sheathed in a robe covered with animal heads which leaves her
breasts bare—a striking image of a fertility goddess.

The Legend of Artemis
She was born a day before her brother Apollo, and she shared the
vicissitudes which marked the childhood of her brother, accompanying
him on his expedition against the serpent Python and during his exile.
As soon as she was born she asked her father Zeus, not for ornaments or
jewellery but a short tunic, hunting boots, a bow and quiver full of
arrows.

In the savage mountain region of Arcadia, Artemis accompanied by
six young Oceanids and twenty nymphs, who were appointed to the
care of her pack of swift hounds, gave herself to the pleasure of the
chase. She was as skilled as her brother when she bent her bow of
sparkling gold and let fly her deadly arrows.

In her outdoor existence there was no place for love. To the virgin
huntress even the legitimate joys of marriage were repugnant, and she
made of chastity a strict law which she imposed on her companions.
The unfortunate Callisto who was approached and seduced by Zeus
in the guise of the goddess herself fell beneath Artemis's wrath when
her disgrace became known.

Then there was the story of Actaeon (see p. 45). On one occasion
Artemis was deeply attracted to the hunter Orion. Perhaps she was in
love with him and she might even have married him. However, he
died and there are two versions of his death.

First: Orion was a strong swimmer and swam far out to sea, so far
that he almost vanished from view. That day Apollo challenged his
sister to hit the scarcely perceptible point, which moved far out on the
surface of the waves. Artemis, not realising that the distant object was
Orion, accepted the challenge, bent her bow and shot an arrow. It
pierced the temple of her loved one. (Did Apollo wish to safeguard his
sister's honour, or was he motivated by a secret jealousy?)

Second: It is said that Orion perished for having dared to touch
the goddess one day when they were hunting together in the Island of

Chios. Artemis summoned a deadly scorpion from the earth which stung Orion on the heel.

The choice of version is yours.

The death of the Aliodaes is attributed to her. The two giants attempted to violate her and Artemis turned herself into a white doe and placed herself between them in such a way that when trying to strike the beast with their javelins they ran each other through instead. Artemis killed Chione, whom her brother Apollo loved, because Chione was vain of her children's beauty, also because she loved Hermes and Apollo on the same night. When she was killed by the goddess, Chione was changed into a hawk.

Niobe, who had twelve children, was punished because she taunted Leto for having only two children (Apollo and Artemis). So Artemis struck Niobe's children with her arrows. Niobe was so heartbroken that she persuaded Zeus to change her into a rock.

The slightest negligence towards Artemis was apt to be punished: Admetus who had omitted to offer a sacrifice to the goddess on his marriage, found his bridal chamber full of snakes. Oeneus forgot to consecrate the first fruits of his crop and had his territory ravaged by a prodigious boar—his whole family perished in its capture.

It would be wrong, however, to consider the daughter of Leto completely barbarous, for when she rejoiced, she hung up her bow and dressed in gracious style, led and directed the lovely choir of the muses and graces. She was particularly venerated at Ephesus. The origin of this cult goes back to the Amazons, mythical female warriors who came from the Caucasus. They cut off their right breast in order to use the bow more easily. ('Amazon' means breastless.)

Once a year they would go to their neighbours, the Gargarensians, to form temporary unions, and would only keep the baby girls, who from infancy were trained for the chase and for war. To the Amazons was attributed the foundation of many towns: Smyrna, Ephesus, Cyme, Myrina and Paphos.

ATALANTA AND MELANION (*Plate* 33)

Atalanta was the daughter of the Arcadian Iasus. Iasus had wanted a son and he exposed his infant daughter on Mount Parthenius where she was suckled by a bear, and later taken in and looked after by the hunters whose rough life she shared. Her greatest pleasure was the chase, and she took an illustrious part in Meleager's boar hunt.

Her father wanted her to marry, but she declared that she would only marry the man who could beat her in a foot race (to lose against her meant death). Many a suitor had been killed in this way, when a certain Melanion thought of a trick. While he ran he dropped, one by

Plate 33. A fine Mortlake Tapestry depicting Atalanta and Melanion, circa 1700
(See page 60)

one, three golden apples which Aphrodite had given him. Atalanta paused to pick them up, was beaten and married Melanion. The couple were turned into lions for having profaned a temple of Zeus.

ATHENE

The Birth of Athene

When Zeus swallowed his wife Metis, she was just about to give birth to a child. Shortly afterwards, Zeus was tortured by an intolerable pain in his head. To be cured, he called his son Hephaestus to split open his skull with a bronze axe, and from the gaping wound, shouting a triumphant victory cry, sprang the child of Zeus and Metis, called Athene, and she was fully armed and brandishing a sharp javelin. At the sight of this, all immortals were struck with astonishment and awe.

Athene loved and showed particular benevolence to the land of Attica. It was because of this that Athens was named after her. There on the Acropolis stands the remains of her temple where she was highly venerated throughout the ages by all. Today the Acropolis of Athens is one of the most popular tourist attractions.

61

Athene and Poseidon disputed the possession of Athens, and to affirm his rights, Poseidon struck the rock of the Acropolis and salt water streamed forth. Athene in her turn caused an olive tree to sprout on the Acropolis, a tree which could be seen in the time of Pericles, still alive after having been burned by the Persians. Zeus gave favour to Athene in the dispute.

Athene protected the brave and valorous. She helped the following heroes: Hercules, Perseus, Bellerophon, Odysseus, Jason, and Telemachus, and took great pains to see them through their trials and tribulations. Athene was benevolent in peace and rendered valuable services to mankind. She taught the people of Cyrene the art of taming horses, helped Jason to build the Argo, and invented the potter's wheel. Her embroidery was unsurpassed. Arachne challenged her skill and the goddess was so furious because she could find no fault in the maiden's work that she changed her into a spider (see *Arachne*, p. 57). In Boeotia they attributed the flute to Athene. She was also known as the Goddess of Health, and extended her protection not only to individuals but to entire cities.

Athene was kindly disposed towards Bellerophon. She appeared to him in a dream and gave him a golden bridle, thanks to which he was able to tame the winged horse Pegasus. Bellerophon perished when he tried to fly to heaven on Pegasus.

The name Athene Parthenos was given by Phidias to the gold and ivory statue which once stood in the Parthenon. (Parthenos means virgin.) Athene was insensitive to the pangs of love, and she defended her virginity fiercely. One day Teiresias by chance saw Athene bathing. The goddess was so furious that she deprived Teiresias of his sight. The other gods were very upset with Athene's behaviour, and asked her to revoke her decision, but Athene would not change her mind. However, Zeus conferred on Teiresias the gift of foretelling the future. Athene had a great love for children and brought up her brother Hephaestus' son Erichthonius who later became king of Athens, where he established the solemn cult of Athene.

Athene's attributes were the helmet, javelin and shield with the gorgon Medusa's head displayed in the centre.

BELLEROPHON
Son of Glaucus and Eurymede.

Bellerophon was one of the seven great destroyers of monsters. Athene gave him a golden bridle, which enabled him to tame Pegasus.

One day, Bellerophon went to the palace of King Proetus. The King's wife, Stheneboea, at once fell in love with Bellerophon. He scorned her, and she was so upset that she told her husband that he had attempted to seduce her. King Proetus did not dare to kill a man who was his guest, so he sent Bellerophon to his father-in-law, Iobates, with a sealed message containing his death sentence.

Iobates imposed various tasks on Bellerophon, hoping he would thus perish. The first task was to fight the Chimaera. With the help of the winged horse Pegasus, Bellerophon flew over the Chimaera and stuffed the monster's jaws with lead. The lead melted in the flames which the Chimaera vomited forth and killed it. The next task was against the Amazons, in which Bellerophon again triumphed. Iobates heard of his success and sent his strongest man to lie in ambush, but Bellerophon killed the man. Iobates was so filled with admiration that he gave the hero his daughter's hand in marriage.

Plate 34. A fine Mortlake Tapestry depicting Arcas and Callisto, circa 1700 (See page 64)

The end of Bellerophon's life was tragic. His two children were slain, one by Ares and the other by Artemis. He was so overcome with sadness at the death of his children that he mounted Pegasus and tried to fly to heaven, and in this way perished.

CALLISTO AND ARCAS (Plate 34)

Callisto was one of Artemis' warriors, and as such did not spend her time spinning wool or arranging her hair. She was very beautiful and wore a tunic pinned together with a brooch, her hair carelessly caught back with a white ribbon, and in her hand a light javelin or bow. The sight of her kindled the fire of passion in the very marrow of the bones of Zeus.

One day when she entered a grove alone and laid down to rest, Zeus saw her, tired and unprotected, and assuming the appearance and the dress of Artemis (Diana), he spoke to the girl. 'Dearest of all my companions', he said, 'where have you been hunting? On what mountain ridges?' 'Greetings divine mistress', she cried. He kissed her but not with the restraint becoming of a maiden's kisses; and entreated her to tell of her hunting exploits in the forest. Who could defeat Zeus? He had his way and returned to the upper air. The maiden was filled with loathing for the groves and woods that had witnessed her fall. Later she met Artemis (Diana) and her companions, who decided to undress and bathe in the brook. All bathed except Callisto who blushed and as she hesitated the others pulled off her tunic, thus revealing at one and the same time her body and her crime. Callisto stood dismayed. Artemis cried 'Off with you! Do not defile this sacred Spring!' and ordered her to withdraw from her company.

The wife of the mighty Zeus, Hera, had long since realised what had happened and was resolved to inflict stern punishment—already a child, Arcas, had been born to her rival and this in itself enraged her. She seized her rival and turned her into a bear—but left her mind unchanged. Often Callisto forgot what she had become and hid when she saw wild beasts. Though a bear herself she shuddered at the sight of other bears.

Meanwhile her son Arcas had reached the age of fifteen, and was unaware of what had happened to his mother. One day he was engaged in tracking wild beasts when he came face to face with her. She stopped when she saw Arcas and seemed to recognise him, but he, not knowing the reason for such behaviour, shrank back, terrified at the beast which gazed at him so fixedly, never taking its eyes off him. As she tried in her eagerness to approach him, he would have pierced her heart with an arrow or his deadly spear, but the almighty Zeus stayed his hand and prevented the crime being committed by removing both mother and son. A whirlwind carried them off into the sky as

Love

Plate 5. The Tapestry Room, Osterley Park House

Plate 6. The Grape Harvest

Plate 7. Hawking

Aesclepius the Healer

Plate 9. The Ten Virgins

neighbouring constellations: Callisto, The Great Bear, and Arcas, as The Little Bear (located in the heavens behind his mother as her guardian).

CASSANDRA (ALEXANDRA)
One of the twelve daughters of King Priam and Hecuba of Troy.

Cassandra was the most beautiful of King Priam's daughters, and was courted by many princes. Apollo fell in love with Cassandra, and promised that if she would yield herself to him he would confer upon her the gift of prophecy. Cassandra asked for the powers of prophecy first, and Apollo agreed. She then refused to yield to him. Apollo begged for just a single kiss, which was granted. In this way he breathed into her mouth, and although he left her with the powers of foretelling the future, he took away her powers of persuasion, so that from then onwards no one would believe what Cassandra predicted.

Her disregarded prophecies were:
1. If Paris went to Sparta, Troy would be destroyed (Paris abducted Helen from Sparta).
2. Troy would fall.
3. There were Greeks in the Trojan horse.
4. That her mother Hecuba would change into a bitch.
5. She would be carried away into slavery.
6. The death of Agamemnon.
7. Agamemnon's son, Orestes, would avenge the death of his father.

CEPHALUS AND PROCRIS (*Plate* 35)
Cephalus had just married Procris, whom he dearly loved, when Eos saw him hunting and she carried him off to Syria. Far from responding to the goddess's love, Cephalus thought only of his beloved Procris. Eos filled him with doubts of his wife's fidelity and advised him to test her. Cephalus then approached Procris in disguise, and, offering her rich jewels, tried to seduce her. Procris repelled him at first but finally the temptation was too strong for her. Cephalus revealed his identity and drove her away.

The unhappy Procris retired to Euboea, where she met Artemis to whom she told her story. Artemis gave her a dog that never lost its scent and a javelin which never missed its mark, and sent her back in disguise to Cephalus to test him. This time, Cephalus was offered the dog and the javelin and when he was tempted he made the same mistake his wife had previously made. The couple then became reconciled. But Procris still feared that her husband might be unfaithful to her and followed him when he went hunting, spying on him without his suspecting it. One day when Procris was hidden in a thicket, Cephalus heard a rustling sound and thinking it was a wild beast he

Plate 35. A fine Mortlake Tapestry depicting Cephalus and Procris, circa 1700
(See page 65)

threw the javelin which never missed its mark. Procris was slain and Cephalus was inconsolable, and retired alone to the island of Cephallenia (named after him).

CHLORIS (FLORA) (*Plate 36*)
Chloris (Flora) was the Greek and Roman Goddess of Flowers. She married Zephyrus, God of Winds and was the mother of Nestor, eleven other sons and one daughter. The Romans celebrated her Festival of Flowers on the first of May. To commemorate famous men who died and were reborn or metamorphosed, flowers were used in the festival: e.g., Anemone, Hyacinth, Narcissus. The triumph of Chloris (Flora) depicts them all.

66

Circe was the daughter of the Sun God, Helios (Hyperion) and Perseis.

Circe married a prince of Colchis whom she murdered, in order to obtain his kingdom. She was expelled by her subjects and carried by her father to the island of Aeaea.

Circe was an enchantress, and was celebrated for her knowledge of magic and poisonous herbs. She used her skill for evil purposes and was noted for her cruelty.

This beautiful sorceress touched all her visitors, invariably male, with her magic wand, turning them into swine. Odysseus landed on Aeaea on his way home from Troy, and his men were turned into swine, but he protected himself from her magic by taking a strange drug called 'moly', which was given to him by Hermes. He forced Circe to give him back his men who had all been turned into swine. Odysseus stayed a while with Circe and she had a son by him, Telegonus.

It is said that Circe married Telemachus, son of Odysseus. They lived near Rome and she was worshipped as a goddess by the Romans.

Plate 36. A fine Royal Brussels Tapestry depicting the crowning of Chloris (See page 66)

DAEDALUS AND ICARUS

Daedalus was accused of treachery for helping Ariadne and Theseus, who killed the Minotaur. So King Minos locked up Daedalus and his son Icarus in the Labyrinth.

Daedalus, who invented the saw and the axe, among other things, contrived to make two pairs of wings with feathers and wax. When completed they flew to freedom.

Icarus flew too near the sun and it melted the wax. He plummeted on to the rocks of the sea shore below, and is remembered in the name, the Icarian Sea. Daedalus landed in Cumae and fled to Sicily where he became a guest and friend of King Cocalus. King Minos pursued Daedalus and when he reached Cumae demanded that Daedalus be handed over to him. King Cocalus refused, and was so angry that King Minos could dare to break the code of honour, that he had his men drown King Minos in his bath.

DANAE AND ZEUS

Danae's father, Acrisius, was told by an oracle that one day his daughter would bring into the world a son by whose hand he would perish. He therefore locked up Danae in a tower with her nurse. But Zeus, who was attracted by the girl's beauty, found a way to enter the chamber. He took the form of a 'shower of gold', and frequently visited Danae.

The result was the birth of a son, Perseus. Acrisius was terrified of this miraculous birth, and shut up both mother and child in a chest which he cast out to sea. Tossed by the waves, the chest was carried out to the island of Seriphus, where a fisherman called Dictys (who was the brother of King Polydectes) caught it in his net. Danae and Perseus were found alive and well inside the chest.

DEMETER (CERES)

Daughter of Coronus and Rhea. Mother of Pluto (Hades) by Iasion; also mother of Persephone by Zeus.

Demeter was one of the twelve great Olympians. She was Goddess of Agriculture, productive soil, fruit, fullness of mankind, Guardian of Marriage and Goddess of Wealth.

Demeter's daughter Persephone was picking flowers one day. Suddenly the earth opened and Pluto, the Ruler of the Dead, came up from Hades in his chariot. He seized Persephone and took her down to the realm of the dead. Persephone cried out to her mother but to no avail, as Zeus had destined the girl to become the Queen of the Dead. Demeter heard the cry from her daughter and began to search for her.

For nine days she wandered the earth, day and night, and could not find Persephone anywhere. Helios, the Sun, told Demeter of the decree of Zeus, and this made Demeter so angry that she left the company of the gods on Olympus, and furthermore she withheld the growth of all vegetation. There was a famine and the gods were deprived of the honour of sacrifices because of the wrath of Demeter. So Zeus sent Iris his messenger, followed by all the other gods to ask Demeter to rejoin the immortals, but she would not listen, and said that she would not return or allow the fruits to grow until she saw her daughter again.

Pluto was asked by Zeus to allow Persephone to go up to see her mother Demeter. Pluto (Hades) agreed to this, but gave Persephone a sweet seed of a pomegranate to eat, so that she would have to return to Hades again. Hermes was sent down with his steeds and chariots and brought back Persephone from the realm of darkness, and mother and daughter rejoiced. Zeus then decreed that Persephone should stay with Demeter on earth for one-third of the year and for two-thirds of the year should return to Hades to be Pluto's Queen in the kingdom of the dead.

Then Demeter walked over the barren land making it fruitful again. Demeter taught men how to plough fields and Hephaestus made her a sickle with which she showed them how to cut corn.

DIDO (ELISSA)
Daughter of the King of Tyre.

Dido went to Africa where she founded Carthage and became its Queen. Aeneas came to Carthage, on his way to Italy after the Trojan War, and Dido fell in love with him.

When Aeneas left for Italy in fulfilment of his divine mission to become the ancestor of the Roman Empire, Dido stabbed herself on a funeral pyre in her despair.

DIONYSUS (BACCHUS) (*Plate* 37)
The God of Wine, Vegetation and Warm Moisture.
Dionysus was the son of Zeus and the Theban princess Semele. He was the only god whose parents were not both divine.

His head with its long curly hair is crowned with vine leaves and bunches of grapes. In one hand he holds a grape or a cup of wine, in the other a thyrsus (staff tipped with ornaments like a pine-cone). Grown to manhood he wandered to far-off places and everywhere he taught men the culture of his vine and the mysteries of his worship. Everywhere they accepted him as a god.

The God of Wine could be kind and beneficent; he could also be cruel and drive men to frightful deeds. Often he made them mad. The Maenads, or the Bacchantes as they were sometimes called, were women frenzied with wine who would tear to pieces the wild creatures they met and devour them.

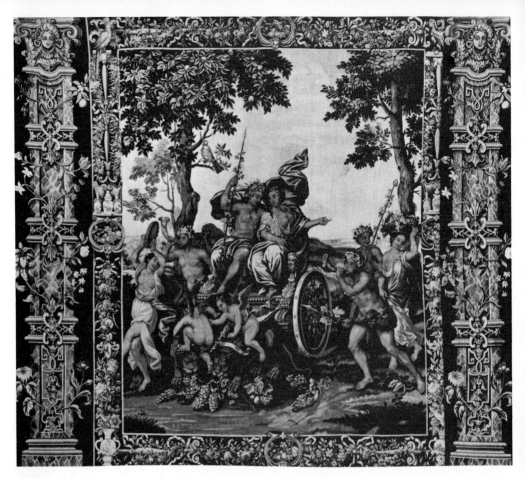

Plate 37. A fine Soho Tapestry depicting Dionysus and Ariadne, circa 1720
(See story of Theseus, page 127, and Dionysus, page 69)

Dionysus's wine could either give his worshippers his blessing or their ruin (the god was a benefactor or a destroyer). Under his influence, courage was quickened and fear vanished, so that people felt about him as about no other god. He was not only outside them, but within them too. They felt that they too could be transformed, and that they themselves could become divine.

ECHO AND NARCISSUS (*Plate* 38)
Narcissus was a beautiful youth, yet he for his part cared for nobody but himself. There lived at the same time as Narcissus, a maiden called Echo, who fell in love with him, and although she was beautiful Narcissus did not care for her. In despair she wandered off into the mountains and pined until she died—all but her voice, which remained to warn other maidens not to fall in love with people who could never return their love.

Aphrodite (Venus), the Goddess of Love, had seen poor Echo's trouble, and angry with Narcissus she was determined to punish him. So one day as Narcissus was bending down to drink water from a clear forest pool, she made him catch sight of his own reflection in the water, and made him think that it was some beautiful water nymph. He tried to catch the reflection, but as soon as he touched the water the surface was ruffled and the face disappeared. Day and night he stayed by the pool trying to capture his love, until he too pined away and died of love and despair. And so poor Echo was avenged.

When Narcissus died the gods changed him into the beautiful pale flower which has ever since borne his name.

EOS (AURORA) (*Plate 39*)
Goddess of Dawn.

Eos sometimes appears as a winged goddess tilting an urn from which falls morning dew. Sometimes she is mounted on the horse Pegasus and bears in her hand a torch. Most often, saffron-robed Eos rode a purple chariot drawn by two horses. She conceived a passion for

Plate 38. A fine Mortlake Tapestry depicting Echo and Narcissus, circa 1700 (See page 70)

Plate 39.   A fine Beauvais Tapestry depicting Eos carrying away Orion the
hunter, circa 1750 (See page 71)

Plate 40.   A fine Paris Tapestry depicting the Zephyr bearing Psyche's two sisters to her palace, circa 1650 (See page 74)

Orion the hunter, whom she carried off and kept with her to the great annoyance of the gods. Artemis finally killed Orion by accident. (See *Artemis*, p. 59). Eos also conceived a passion for Cephalus, and carried him off to Syria. (See *Cephalus and Procris*, p. 65.)

EROS (CUPID) AND PSYCHE (*Plate* 40)

Eros was the youngest of all the gods; he was winged, gracious, but rebellious and his pranks caused much suffering among gods and men. His father was Zeus, and his mother Aphrodite.

Psyche was very beautiful. Aphrodite was jealous of her, and she commanded Psyche's father, through an oracle, to take his daughter to a solitary rock to await her fate, which was to become the prey of a monster. Psyche was duly left on the rock, and trembling she awaited the fulfilment of the oracle. Suddenly she felt herself carried off in the arms of Zephyrus, The West Wind, who took her away to a magnificent palace. Night came and Psyche was on the verge of sleep, when a mysterious being joined her in the darkness, explaining he was to be her husband. She could not see him, but his voice was soft and his conversation full of tenderness.

Before dawn he made Psyche swear never to attempt to see his face. For the maiden, life was suddenly wonderful and her happiness could have continued so had it not been for her sisters, who were consumed by envy and sowed the seeds of suspicion in her heart. They nagged her so much that one night she stealthily lit a lamp and held it above the mysterious face. Instead of the monster her sister had made her expect, she saw Eros himself. A drop of oil fell on the god's shoulder, and he awoke at once, reproaching Psyche for her lack of faith, then immediately vanished. The palace likewise vanished, and poor Psyche found herself on a lonely rock again, in the midst of terrifying solitude.

From then on she was pursued by Aphrodite's anger, and subjected to a series of terrible ordeals. These Psyche managed to overcome thanks to a mysterious assistance. Her last task was to descend to the Underworld and ask Persephone for a box containing a magic ointment which would keep its user young and beautiful forever. The journey was indeed terrible. At the gateway of the Underworld stood the three-headed dog, Cerberus, ready to tear all-comers limb from limb. Zephyrus advised Psyche to take food with her, which she should throw to each of the three heads in order to pass safely, and she followed his instructions. So sweet and gentle and sad was she that Persephone's heart was filled with pity and even the stern Pluto smiled. They gave her the box that Aphrodite had asked for, and set her on her way back.

Plate 41. A fine Gobelin Tapestry depicting the story of Europa and the bull, circa 1720 (See page 76). The top border shows the Arms of Scott, Baronet of Kew Gardens

When she reached the upper world, she was exhausted by all the trials and difficulties she had undergone, and decided that there could be no harm in taking just a little of the ointment to bring back some of her loveliness. She opened the lid of the box, meaning to put some of the ointment on her face. But the box contained nothing but the spirit of sleep, which is more powerful than anything in the world to restore beauty, and when Psyche opened the lid, a deep sleep fell on her and she sank by the wayside, sorrows and pain forgotten.

Eros flew in search of her. He had convinced his mother that Psyche had suffered enough, and that she had won the right to love and happiness again. He bent down and woke her with a kiss. He spoke tender words of reassurance to her, promising to love her forever, then she drank from the cup of life and became immortal. Aphrodite blessed them both.

EUROPA AND ZEUS (*Plate* 41)
Europa was the daughter of Agenor, King of Phoenicia.

The Rape of Europa
One day Europa was gathering flowers with her companions when she caught sight of a bull with a glistening hide, who browsed peacefully among her father's herd. His air was gentle and yet at the same time majestic. She did not suspect that this bull was none other than the master of the gods, Zeus himself, who had assumed this shape in order to deceive the girl of whom he had become enamoured. Trustingly, Europa approached and caressed the animal, who very gallantly knelt before her. She began to wreath flowers around its powerful horns and then climbed playfully onto his mighty back. Suddenly the bull reared to its feet, raced towards the sea and sprang into the waves, carrying the weeping virgin across the vast sea to Crete.

They sheltered under a plane tree where Zeus made Europa his mistress. Because the tree witnessed the divine union it retained its foliage in all seasons. Europa gave birth to three sons, Minos, Sarpedon, and Rhadamanthys. All three were adopted by the King of Crete, Asterius, who subsequently became Europa's husband.

FATES (THE PARCAE)
The Moerae
1. Clotho—the spinner who personified the thread of life.
2. Lachesis—chance, the element of luck man had the right to expect.
3. Atropos—inescapable fate, against which there was no appeal.

The three Moerae arrived at man's birth. They had to be invoked when he married, so that the union should be happy, and finally when the end approached they hastened to cut the thread of his life.

Nemesis
Like the Fates, Nemesis had at first been a Moral Idea, that of the inexorable equilibrium of human conditions: Firstly, Man could displease the gods by offending the Moral Law; secondly, by attaining too much happiness or riches and exciting their jealousy. In either of these cases the imprudent mortal was pursued by Nemesis or the Divine Anger.

Tyche, Ate, Litae
Tyche—was the Goddess of Fortune. She wears attributes of abundance adorned with a crown.
Ate—was a malevolent creature who prompted men to irresponsible acts, and led both men and gods into error. Hence, Zeus banished the wicked goddess from Olympus, and flung her into the midst of man's affairs.
Litae—Zeus sent the Litae after Ate in order to repair the damage she had done. The Litae were Prayers and also the daughters of Zeus. Wrinkled and lame, they limped after their sister Ate, attempting to mitigate the evils she caused. Whoever welcomed the Litae with respect was showered with blessings.

THE FOUR AGES OF MAN
First Age: The Golden Age
Men lived like gods, free from worry and fatigue; old age did not afflict them; they rejoiced in continual festivity. Their lot did not include immortality, but at least they died as though overcome by sweet slumber. All the blessings of the world were theirs, the fruitful earth gave forth its treasures unbidden. At their death men of the Golden Age became benevolent genii, protectors and guardians of the living.

Second Age: The Silver Age
During this age there lived a race of feeble and inept men, who obeyed their mothers all their lives (The Matriarchal Age). They were also agriculturalists.

Third Age: The Bronze Age
The men of the Bronze Age were robust as ash trees, and delighted only in oaths and warlike exploits. Their pitiless hearts were as hard as steel; their might was untameable; their arms invincible. They ended by mutually cutting each other's throats. From this generation, however, dated the discovery of the first metals, and the first attempts at civilisation.

Plate 42.   A fine 17th Century Brussels Tapestry depicting the story of Ganymede
(See page 79)

Fourth Age: The Iron Age
The Contemporary Age, a period of misery and crime, 'When men respected neither their vows, nor justice, nor virtue'.

This is how the Greeks explained the progressive degeneration of mankind.

78

GANYMEDE (*Plate* 42)

He is depicted as an adolescent in a Phrygian cap, a mantle thrown back over his shoulders, either seated beside Zeus or carried through the air by an eagle.

In spite of the honorary position he occupied on Olympus, Ganymede was not of divine birth, being the son of Tros, King of Phrygia, and of Callirrhoe. He was distinguished among mortals for his extraordinary beauty. Zeus was charmed, and wishing to make him his favourite, had him swept up by his eagle from the plains of Troad and brought to Olympus. It was also said that Zeus himself took the form of an eagle in order to carry off the fair adolescent. To recompense Tros for the loss of his son, Zeus, presented him with magnificent steeds, 'swift as the storm'. On Olympus, Ganymede became the cup-bearer of the gods, and his beauty rejoiced the eyes of all.

THE GRACES

The three Graces, fathered by Zeus, were smiling divinities whose presence spread joy, not only throughout the external world, but also in the hearts of men. Their names were, *Aglaia, Euphrosyne* and *Thalia*.

They were Aphrodite's companions and attended to her toilet. The goddess made use of their services when she wished to adorn herself in all her seductions. With the return of spring, the Graces delighted in mingling with the nymphs. This was because these divinities—in whom some have seen a personification of the sun's rays, but who were originally nature goddesses—also presided over budding of plant-life, and the ripening of fruits. Aglaia, was 'the brilliant'. Thalia, was 'she who brought flowers'. The joy which results from the sun's blessings is revealed in Euphrosyne's name—'she who rejoices the heart'.

In origin as well as function, the Graces were closely connected with Apollo: hence they often form part of his retinue. They were also considered to be Goddesses of Gratitude. Thus their mother was sometimes said to be Lethe (Oblivion) because gratitude is quickly forgotten.

HADES (PLUTO)

Hades also means 'House of Hell and Underworld'. Hades is the ruler over the kingdom of the dead. Hades, like other gods, has a chariot but his steeds are always black and he uses golden reins. Hades is the God of Agriculture and from the centre of the earth he exerts his influence on cultivation.

He is depicted with a helmet or mask in his hand which would make him invisible if he wished to emerge from the Underworld unseen.

Plants which are sacred to him are the cypress and narcissus. One day Persephone was gathering flowers from a green meadow when she saw a beautiful narcissus; as she picked it the earth opened and Hades appeared in all his glory with his chariot and black steeds with golden reins. He carried her off to be his Queen in the Underworld. (See *Demeter*, p. 68.)

HECTOR (*End paper*)

Hector was the eldest son of King Priam of Troy. He married Andromache and they had a son called Astyanax.

As King Priam was very old the chief burden of defending Troy against the Greeks fell on Hector. The siege lasted ten years (1194–1184 B.C.) and was caused by Hector's youngest brother Paris who carried off Helen, the wife of King Menelaus (see *Judgement of Paris*, p. 113).

King Menelaus brought many famous Greek fighters to Troy to regain his wife Helen. Among his helpers were King Agamemnon, Achilles, Odysseus, Nestor, Patroclus, the two Ajaxes, Calchas and many others.

Hector at first advised Paris to return Helen to King Menelaus her husband, but his advice was rejected. Next, he tried to arrange a duel

Plate 43.   A fine 17th Century Aubusson Tapestry depicting Helen of Troy arriving home with the plunder of war, escorted by her husband, King Menelaus and King Agamemnon (See page 81)

between Paris and King Menelaus as he considered the whole thing to be a private affair, but this was interrupted by Athena.

Hector was honoured by his people and respected by the Greeks for his courage. He was the chief hero who engaged in battle the bravest of the Greeks, and killed no fewer than thirty-one of them including Patroclus, Achilles' friend.

Achilles in turn, infuriated by the death of his friend Patroclus, slew Hector and dragged his corpse three times around the walls of Troy. After the death of Hector, with the help of Hermes, King Priam redeemed his son's body and brought it back to Troy for burial. Troy fell to the Greeks. Hector's son Astyanax was hurled from the walls of Troy by Odysseus, and his beautiful wife Andromache was taken as a slave by Neoptolemus.

HELEN OF TROY (*Plates* 43, 44)
Daughter of Zeus and Leda.

Zeus took the form of a swan to seduce Leda. That same night she slept with her husband. Some time after these unions she gave birth to two eggs, each containing two children. One of these children was Helen, the most beautiful woman of the age. Twenty-seven princes of Greece sought her hand. She chose Menelaus, King of Sparta, and had one daughter, Hermione. Later Helen was abducted by the Trojan Paris, to whom she had been promised by Aphrodite because Paris had awarded Aphrodite the Golden Apple (see *Judgement of Paris,* p. 113). The abduction of Helen was the cause of the Trojan War (see *Hector,* p. 80).

HEPHAESTUS (VULCAN) (*Plate* 45)
Son of Zeus and Hera.

Hephaestus was the God of Fire and is depicted as a robust black-smith, with a bearded face, powerful neck and hairy chest. In his hands he grasps a hammer.

Hephaestus was a lame and deformed god, and it is said that the cause of this was that Zeus kicked him out of Olympus to the island of Lemnos. Aphrodite was his wife and was unfaithful to him (see *Ares and Aphrodite,* p. 57). Hephaestus's son by Aphrodite was Eros.

Hephaestus is famous for the following creations as a blacksmith.
1. The arms of Achilles
2. The arms of Aeneas
3. The shield of Hercules
4. The necklace of Hermione, a gift which proved fatal to all who wore it

Plate 44. 16th Century Brussels Tapestry of the History of Troy. Ulysses and Diomed are depicted with King Priam in the background. Judgement of Paris (See pages 81 and 113)

5. The sceptre of Agamemnon
6. The steel net which trapped his wife Aphrodite, and Ares.
7. The arrows of Apollo and Artemis
8. Demeter's sickle
9. Pandora's golden crown

He was helped in his work by the Cyclops. Hephaestus was patron of all artists who work with iron and metals.

HERA (JUNO) *(Plate 65)*

The eldest daughter of Cronus and Rhea, born on the island of Samos.

Hera's childhood was spent on the isle of Euboea, where her brother Zeus found her and made her his wife. All the immortals rejoiced at Hera's marriage to Zeus on Olympus, and the Fates themselves chanted the hymenal chorus.

Hera had four children: the gracious Hebe; Ilithyia, mother of birth pangs; the impetuous Ares; the skilful Hephaestus. She was always faithful to Zeus, and he was constantly unfaithful.

Every year Hera went to bathe in the spring Camathus at Nauplia, and in these waters renewed her virginity. The goddess was irresistible when she anointed her body with an oil whose sweetness was such that the heavens and earth were filled with its fragrance.

Plate 45.   A fine Brussels Tapestry depicting Hephaestus making the arms of Achilles, circa 1650 (See page 81)

Hera would never have lacked suitors, had she wished them. King Ixion, when invited to dine with the gods, was inflamed with an all-consuming desire for her. Zeus chastised Ixion for his insolence by binding him to a fiery wheel which whirled him perpetually through the sky.

Hera was unable to control Zeus, but she could at least vent her fury on her rivals.

Hera was the Goddess of Marriage and Maternity, and represented the idealised wife. She is depicted as a chaste and rather severe beauty. Her attributes are a sceptre surmounted by a cuckoo, the pomegranate and the peacock.

Hera, like Zeus, was venerated on the summits of mountains. The chief centre of her cult was Argos, where she had six temples. It was Heraeum in Argo which housed the famous statue of Hera, executed by Polycletus, in ivory and gold. The goddess was seated on a throne, her brow crowned by a diadem on which were depicted the Horae and the Graces. In her left hand she held a pomegranate, and in her right a sceptre surmounted by a cuckoo. (See *Io and Zeus*, p. 91.)

Hera also possessed sanctuaries at Mycenae, Olympus, Sparta, Attica, Boetia and Euboea. She was particularly venerated in Crete and Samos, where stood the greatest of her temples.

(See also *Judgement of Paris*, p. 113; *Io and Zeus*, p. 91; *Hercules*, p. 84; *Semele and Zeus*, p. 126.)

HERCULES (*Plate 46 and Front end paper*)
Son of Zeus and Alcmene (see *Alcmene and Zeus*, p. 48).

Zeus destined his son to be King of Mycenae and deliver mankind from the various monsters which dwelt on the earth, and thereafter to become immortal. Hera was jealous of Alcmene and hated Hercules from the moment he was born. When Hercules was eight months old Hera sent a pair of snakes to destroy him but Hercules strangled them, one in each hand.

Hera still wanted revenge and inspired Hercules into a fit of madness in which he killed his own children. For his punishment Hercules was ordered by the Oracle of Delphi to carry out twelve labours to be imposed by Eurystheus King of Mycenae.

The Labours
1. To bring back the skin of the Nemean lion whose hide he afterwards wore.
2. To kill the Hydra of Lerna. As he severed each of the water-snakes nine heads he cauterised the bleeding necks to prevent re-growth. The beast's gall was used thenceforth to poison Hercules' arrows.

Plate 46. A fine 17th Century Brussels Tapestry depicting the first task of Hercules (See page 84)

3. To capture the Ceryneian stag, which took one year. The stag was one of five, the other four drew the chariot of Artemis. It had golden horns and brazen hooves. The stag had to be captured and brought back alive to Mycenae.

4. He was to bring back alive to Mycenae the wild Erymanthus boar. Hercules caught the boar in deep snow after a long pursuit.

5. He was commanded to clean out the stables of Augeias in one day. He did this by diverting a river, causing the water to pass through the stables.

6. Hercules was told to drive away the Stymphalian birds. These were nursed by Ares. They used their feathers as arrows, had brazen claws and beaks, ate humans and destroyed the crops with their droppings. Hercules found them in Arcadia and drove them off with brazen rattles made by Hephaestus. As they flew away Hercules shot them with his arrows, those who escaped settled on the island of Ares in the Black Sea.

7. Hercules was to bring back to Mycenae the Cretan bull. King Minos had omitted to sacrifice this bull to Poseiden, who then caused it to ravage Crete. The bull swam across the sea from Crete to the Peloponnese with Hercules on its back. At Mycenae Eurystheus, thinking that Hercules had tamed it, let it go free. The bull later devastated the country around Marathon and was afterwards killed by Theseus.

8. Hercules was ordered to bring back to Mycenae the man-eating mares of Diomedes of Thrace. Hercules threw Diomedes, their own master, to the horses. Having devoured him, they lost their fierceness and Hercules was able to drive them aboard his ship, and eventually get them to Eurystheus at Mycenae. Eurystheus dedicated them to Hera, who let them loose on Mount Olympus, where the wild beasts of Apollo destroyed them.

9. Hercules was to bring back the belt (or girdle) of Queen Hippolyta of the Amazons who was the daughter of Ares and Naiad, because Admete, daughter of Eurystheus, desired to own it. Hercules therefore collected a band of men and set sail in a single ship. The Amazons lived on the island of Ares (whom they worshipped) and when Hercules arrived Queen Hippolyta heard Hercules story and decided to give him the belt. But Hera, in the likeness of an Amazon, spread a rumour that Hercules was about to carry off the Queen. The Amazons at once took up arms and in the battle many were killed. Hercules captured Queen Hippolyta and took the belt. Hercules then gave the Queen to Theseus, his best friend, who asked for her life.

10. For his tenth labour, Hercules was ordered to fetch the red cattle of Geryon from Erythia which lay far west of the sea. On his travels

he arrived at the ocean near Tartessus, and erected two columns at either side of the straits, which were called the Columns of Hercules (Gibraltar). Hercules navigated on to Erythia. Now Geryon, the son of Chrysaor and Callirrhoe, had three bodies which were joined at the waist, six legs, six arms, and three heads. He was exceedingly strong. His cattle were watched over by the two-headed dog Orthrus, and Eurytion, son of Ares. Hercules, however, smote the dog with his club, killed Eurytion, and with arrows shot dead Geryon. On his return to Mycenae he was attacked by the natives of Liguria (Southern France) and ran out of arrows. So he prayed to Zeus, and Zeus rained stones from the sky which Hercules threw at his attackers and defeated them. Hercules also killed the two sons of Poseidon who tried to rob him of the cattle. Then Hera dispersed the cattle by sending a gadfly to sting them, but Hercules managed to reassemble them, and at last gave them to Eurystheus.

11. Next, Hercules was commanded to fetch the Golden Apples from the garden of the Hesperides (see *Apples of the Hesperides' Garden*, p. 54.)

On his return to Mycenae he killed the vulture (eagle) which daily tortured Prometheus. When Hercules had freed Prometheus he wreathed himself with olive leaves. The leaves were taken to represent the bonds of Prometheus. In the ancient world people wore wreaths on festive occasions in memory of Prometheus.

12. Finally, Hercules was commanded to bring up the multi-headed dog Cerberus from Hades. Now Hades would allow Hercules to take the Cerberus if he could master the dog without weapons. This Hercules did, and ascended with Cerberus through Troezen where an image of bright-eyed Hercules was afterwards erected. He made himself a wreath which was white on one side and dark on the other. The two colours declared that he had laboured among the living and among the dead. His conquest of Hades is the greatest of all his deeds.

Hercules had other exploits which were lesser labours: 1. Killing a huge lion near Mount Cithaeron; 2. Slaying Cacus, a cattle thief; 3. Crushing Autaeus; 4. Killing Birsiris; 5. Slaying Eryx, a boxer; 6. Accompanying the Argonauts; 7. Assisting in the war against the giants, enabling Zeus to win; 8. Conquering Laomedon and plundering Troy (79 years before the Trojan War); 9. Clearing Queen Ompholis's country, Lydia, of a huge serpent and many robbers; 10. Restoring Tyndareus to the throne of Sparta; 11. Defeating Achelous (by wrestling) for the hand of Deianira; 12. Rescuing Hesione from the sea monster.

Hercules was one of the founders of the Olympic Games.

HERMES (MERCURY)
Son of Zeus and Maia.

Hermes was the Messenger of the Gods. His attributes were a winged helmet and sandals and he always carried a winged staff.

He was responsible for increase in the animal world, Deity of wealth, God of trade, and of travellers, manual skill, oratory and eloquence, of thieves and of the wind, with whose speed he was able to move.

Hermes' Exploits:
1. He invented the lyre and gave it to Apollo, who in turn gave him the Caduceus, a golden staff with wings at the top intertwined with serpents.
2. He stole Apollo's cattle.
3. He invented winged sandals (which are called talaria).
4. He was first to make fire by rubbing sticks together.
5. For making the first offerings of flesh of cattle to Zeus, Zeus gave him his winged cap called 'petasus'.

Plate 47. A 17th Century Mortlake Tapestry signed Francis Crane. Hero finds Leander's body washed up on the Sestos (See page 89)

Plate 48. A fine 17th Century Brussels Tapestry depicting the story of Hestia
(See page 90)

Hermes' Duties
1. Conducting souls of the dead to Hades.
2. Taking the three goddesses to the Judgement of Paris.
3. Killing the Argus.
4. Delivering Ares from his long confinement.
5. Purifying the Danaides.
6. Tying Ixion to the wheel in Hades.
7. Warning Aeneas to hasten to Italy.
8. Advising Calypso to send Odysseus away on a raft.
9. Selling Heracles to Omphale.

HERO AND LEANDER (*Plate* 47)
Hero was a beautiful priestess of Aphrodite at Sestos. At a festival there, Leander saw her and fell in love with her. Thereafter, guided by a torch that Hero placed in her tower, Leander swam from his home at Abydos on the opposite side of the Hellespont to be with his loved one. One stormy night he was drowned, and the next day his body was washed up on Sestos. Hero discovered the dead body, and

89

in grief drowned herself. Some say that she saw his body from the tower, and in her grief and despair she tore her tunic, and in doing so fell from the tower.

HESTIA (*Plate* 48)

Hestia was Goddess of Fire, like Hephaestus who was also a fire divinity. But while Hephaestus represented the firey element in its celestial and subterranean manifestations, Hestia symbolised the household fire and later by analogy, the fire in the centre of the earth.

Hestia was venerated in all Greek towns. She has her altar in every *prytaneum* or public hearth. The Hestia of Delphi was the object of a special cult, because Delphi was believed to occupy the centre of the universe and was, therefore, the common hearth of all Greece. The temples of Hestia were characterised by their circular form.

Plate 49.   A fine Antwerp Tapestry depicting the story of Hippolytus and Phaedra
(See page 91)

Representations of Hestia are rare. She was the oldest of the Olympians and always maintained her precedence. Men understood this well, and when they offered sacrifices, consecrated the first morsels of their victims to Hestia, and in the festivals poured her the first and last libations. On Olympus, Hestia's dignity was unquestioned and her rights as the eldest were recognised. 'In the dwellings of the gods,' says Plato, 'Hestia alone maintains repose.' We only know of her that both Poseidon and Apollo sought her in marriage. In an order to put an end to their attentions, she placed herself under the protection of Zeus, the master of the gods. She touched his head making the vow to remain a virgin forever.

Hestia thus shared with Athene and Artemis the prerogative of chastity. Aphrodite's power never succeeded in overcoming her.

HIPPOLYTUS AND PHAEDRA (*Plate* 49)

Hippolytus was the son of Theseus and Hippolyta.

After the death of Hippolyta, Theseus married Phaedra, daughter of King Minos. After a while Phaedra fell in love with Hippolytus, her stepson, but he constantly rejected her overtures. Phaedra became so angry and humiliated that she falsely accused him of rape. (Some say Phaedra hanged herself and left a note accusing Hippolytus).

Theseus readily believed Phaedra's charges and asked Poseidon to punish his son without hearing Hippolytus's side of the story. Poseidon sent a sea monster which terrified Hippolytus's horses so that they bolted and dragged their master to death under the overturned chariot.

IO AND ZEUS (*Plate* 50)

Io performed the duties of priestess to Hera. Zeus fell in love with her and in order to be with her, he took the form of a cloud. He found Hera to be suspicious, so in order to distract her, he changed Io into a white heifer. Hera pretended to be deceived, and asked Zeus for the heifer as a gift. After gentle persuasion he agreed. Once it was in her possession, she placed the animal under the care of Argus Panoptes, the giant with one hundred eyes. Fifty remained open while the other fifty closed in sleep. Zeus, however, ordered the cunning Hermes to set Io free. Hermes succeeded in charming the giant to sleep, with the sound of his flute and when all his eyes were closed, he then cut off his head.

To honour Argus who had served her, Hera distributed his eyes over the tail of her favourite bird, the Peacock. Hera then sent the gadfly to torture the poor heifer by stinging her. Io fled across the world. She swam the Ionian sea, which took her name. One day, after long suffering, she reached Egypt where, by a simple touch of the hand, Zeus restored her to human form. There she bore a son Epaphus ('the touch').

Plate 50.   A fine Paris Tapestry depicting the story of Io and Zeus, circa 1700
(See page 91)

IXION

Ixion, son of Ares, was to marry Dia, daughter of Eioneus. There was
a quarrel between Ixion and his future father-in-law during which
Eioneus was thrown into a burning ditch and killed. Ixion was forced
to seek refuge with Zeus who offered him a temporary home on
Mount Olympus.

While there, Ixion fell in love with Hera. When Zeus realised this,
he decided to test Ixion's audacity by forming a cloud into the likeness
of Hera and giving it to him. From this strange union, the race of
centaurs was born. Zeus then punished Ixion by having him chained
to a fiery wheel which whirled him perpetually through the sky.

JASON (*Plate* 51)

Son of Aeson and Alcimede of Iolcus in Thessaly.

Aeson was expelled from the kingdom by his half-brother Pelias,
and retired to the country. Whilst he was there he was told that Pelias

was going to kill him and his son Jason, so he fled into the hills. There Aeson left Jason in the care of Cheiron, the Centaur. Jason was brought up by Cheiron who taught him medicine and the skills of war.

Pelias was warned by an oracle to beware of a man who wore only one sandal. Therefore he held a great feast and invited all the men. Jason decided to attend, and on his way there, Hera, in the guise of an old woman, fell in love with Jason and to test him asked that he should carry her across the river Anausus. He did so, and lost a sandal.

When Jason met his uncle at the feast he asked him for his rightful share of the kingdom. Pelias was very disturbed for he saw that Jason only wore one sandal, and remembered the oracle. He therefore told his nephew that he would agree to his conditions if Jason first brought back the Golden Fleece which was in the possession of Aietes, King of Colchis, hoping thereby to rid himself of Jason.

Jason brought together a crowd of heroes to go to Colchis. They built the ship Argo, and the heroes were called the Argonauts. They were; 1. Orpheus; 2. Hercules; 3. Castor; 4. Pollux; 5. Zetes; 6. Calais; 7. Mopsus; 8. Telamon; 9. Hylas; 10. Meleager; 11. Peleus; 12. Asterion; 13. Polyphemus; 14. Iphiclus; 15. Admetus; 16. Erytus; 17. Aethalides; 18. Echion; 19. Coronus; 20. Menoetius; 21. Eurytion; 22. Eritobes; 23. Camethus; 24. Clytius; 25. Iphitus; 26. Butes; 27. Tiphys; 28. Phlias; 29. Talaus; 30. Areius; 31. Nauplius; 32. Idmon.

Plate 51. A fine Paris Tapestry by Audran, depicting Jason cutting down the Golden Fleece, dated 1761 (See page 92)

Jason and the Argonauts (*Plate* 52)

After a number of adventures, the Argonauts reached Colchis. There Jason met King Aietes, who consented to give up the Golden Fleece, but imposed certain conditions. Jason had first to harness a plough with two wild bulls whose hooves were of bronze and breath was of flame. With them he had to plough a four acre field and plant it with dragon's teeth. These presently grew in the form of armed men which he would have to cut down and kill. Jason decided to accept these conditions.

While Jason was with King Aietes, Hera and Athene approached Aphrodite with a single thought in mind, which was how to save Jason. They believed that if Aphrodite's son Eros would loose an arrow at Aietes' daughter Medea, she would fall in love with Jason. Medea was the enchantress, daughter of Aietes and descendant of Helios the Sun God. She was skilled in magic, poisons and medicines. Aphrodite agreed with Hera and Athene, and instructed Eros to loose his love arrow, which he did.

Medea fell in love with Jason and gave him a special ointment which made him become invulnerable to sword or fire. Then she told him that when the dragons' teeth sprang up as armed men to throw a boulder in amongst them; they would fall upon it like famished animals and kill one and other. That was the moment to plunge into the fray himself, having sprinkled his spear, sword and shield with the special ointment to protect his weapons and himself from damage. Finally she said that he must not flinch from the encounter at any moment.

Jason carried out the instructions of Medea, and all went well. Then Aietes refused to keep his word; Medea again helped Jason to vanquish the dragon which guarded the Golden Fleece, and to seize the precious trophy. Both then left Colchis with the Argonauts in haste, pursued by Aietes's son, Apsyrtus, and his men. Aietes warned them not to return without the Golden Fleece.

Apsyrtus knew the islands and area well, and soon Jason was surrounded, and Apsyrtus planned to attack. But Medea realised the situation and decided on a plan to trap her brother. So with the help of Jason, Medea gave the heralds a message for Apsyrtus which would serve as bait. She said that he should meet her at midnight by the temple of Artemis, and she would plan to steal the Golden Fleece and return to Colchis with him. Medea went to the temple and Jason hid in ambush. Presently Apsyrtus, tempted by Medea's treacherous offer, unwisely came unescorted to the temple. There he and his sister agreed on every point, and as Apsyrtus turned to leave, Jason leapt from his hiding place, struck him with his sword and killed him. Medea turned her head and shrank aside. The Argonauts, seeing Jason's

Plate 52.   A fine Paris Tapestry by Audran, depicting Jason and the Bulls, dated 1761 (See page 92)

signal of a burning torch, slaughtered the Colchian crew. In the morning, when the rest of Prince Apsyrtus's fleet learnt of what had happened, they decided to give up the chase and settle down in the surrounding islands.

This enabled the Argonauts to resume their homeward voyage, which took them across the Danube, the ocean, the Libyan desert, the Garden of the Hesperides, the Lake of Phaethon, the Mediterranean, and finally the Argonauts returned to Iolcus. Aeson was still alive, and was rejuvenated by one of Medea's magic philtres. By doing this, they persuaded Jason's uncle Pelias that her charms could rejuvenate him too. Medea used a different charm, and Pelias died. So Jason became King of Iolcus and ruled well for ten years. Medea bore him a son. One day on a visit to Corinth, Jason met Creusa (or Glauce), daughter of King Creon, and he abandoned Medea. Medea avenged herself by sending the new bride a magnificent robe which, when placed over her shoulders, consumed her with inextinguishable flames. Medea then cut the throats of the children she had borne Jason, and fled to Athens where she married King Aegeus.

As for Jason, some say that while he was resting in the shade of the ship Argos, the poop fell on him and crushed him to death.

LEDA AND ZEUS
Zeus, on occasions, did not hesitate to pay court to married women. Thus he fell in love with Leda, the wife of Tyndareus. One evening when the young woman was bathing in a pool, she saw floating majestically towards her a swan of dazzling beauty and whiteness. It was Zeus who came to possess her.

The same night, Leda also lay with her own husband. Later, she bore four children. Pollux and Helen, children of Zeus, and Castor and Clytemnestra, children of Tyndareus.

MARSYAS
Marsyas was a Satyr from Phrygia. One day he picked up a flute which Athena had thrown away. He played it so well that he was convinced that not even Apollo, the God of Music, could do better. Apollo heard the challenge and invited Marsyas to a music contest, the loser to be flayed alive and killed. King Midas and the Muses were asked to be judges. All but King Midas judged Apollo the winner. (See *Midas*, p. 97.)

Apollo inflicted on Marsyas the terrible punishment which he had threatened. He hung him on a pine tree and stripped off his skin and killed him. The Marsyas river flows near the place of Marsyas' death. Some say this is because Apollo relented and turned Marsyas

Plate 10.   The Hunts of Louis Quatorze

Plate 11. The Flight from Egypt

Plate 12.   The conveyance of Saint Etienne's body to Constantinople

Plate 13. The ordination of the deacons

Plate 14.   Wall hanging woven tapestry

Plate 15. Christ in Glory tapestry, Coventry Cathedral

into a river; others say it is because the river was made out of the tears of the nymphs and Satyrs who wept for him.

MEDEA

The magician daughter of King Aietes of Colchis.

After helping Jason to steal the Golden Fleece, she fled with him, delaying her pursuing father by cutting up her brother and throwing pieces into the path of the King's ship. After a few years of marriage, Jason abandoned Medea and their children, to marry a Corinthian princess. Medea sent the new bride a present of a dress. When the princess donned the dress it burst into flames and killed her. Medea then slaughtered her children by Jason, and flew in her chariot which was drawn by winged dragons, to Athens, where she married King Aegeus.

MELEAGER, ATALANTA AND MELANION (*Plates* 33, 53)

Meleager's father Oeneus, once forgot to offer to Artemis the first fruits of his harvest, and the angry goddess sent a monstrous wild boar to ravage Aetolia. Meanwhile, Meleager had become a hero, full of valour. To hunt the monster, Meleager invited all the most celebrated heroes of Greece, among them a young Arcadian woman named Atalanta. The hunt was cruel and hard. Many were killed by the wild boar.

Atalanta was the first to wound it with an arrow in the back, and Meleager finally killed the beast with his spear. A dispute arose among the huntsmen over the remains, which Meleager presented to Atalanta. Meleager's uncles attempted to take the spoils away from her, and he killed them.

Atalanta was the unconscious cause of Meleager's troubles. She herself was suckled by a bear, and later found by hunters whose rough life she shared. She slew the Centaurs who had tried to ravish her. She declared that she would only marry a man who could beat her in a foot race, and if they failed, she would then kill them. Many suitors had been killed, when a certain Melanion thought of a trick. Whilst he ran he dropped, one by one, three golden apples which Aphrodite had given him. Atalanta paused to pick them up, was beaten, and married Melanion. The couple were later turned into lions for having profaned the Temple of Zeus.

MIDAS

Midas was the King of Phrygia. One day some of his peasants captured Silenus, the companion of Dionysus, and brought him before King Midas, who welcomed Silenus as an honoured guest, and looked after him until Dionysus could be found.

Plate 53.   A fine Brussels Tapestry depicting 'The Wild Boar of Aetolia', circa 1780 (See story of Meleager, Atalanta and Melanion on page 97)

For his trouble Dionysus granted him a wish. So King Midas asked that whatever he touched might become gold. The wish was fulfilled. King Midas soon regretted his request for everything he touched turned to gold including food, drink, a tree and even his daughter. So he begged to be rid of his gift. Dionysus told him to wash in the river Pactolus, he did so, and ever since the river has had golden sands.

King Midas was made the judge in the music contest between Apollo and Marsyas, and because he judged Marsyas's music sweeter, Apollo changed King Midas's ears into those of an ass.

THE MUSES
Daughters of the King of the gods, Zeus.

It was told after the defeat of the Titans, the gods had asked Zeus to create divinities, who were capable of celebrating the victory of the Olympians. The master of the gods then went to Pieria, where he shared Mnemosyne's couch for nine consecutive nights. When her time came, she gave birth to nine daughters, who formed the choir of the Muses.

The Muses were for long an indissoluble choir, which presided over music and poetry in general. Later a special province was assigned to each:
1. *Clio*—The Muse of history, whose attributes were the heroic trumpet and the ancient time-measuring device, worked by the flow of water (Clepsydra).
2. *Euterpe*—Presided over flute playing, and her attribute was the flute.
3. *Thalia*—First considered a bucolic Muse, and later became the Muse of comedy. In her hands she carried the shepherd's staff and a comic mask.
4. *Melpomene*—The Muse of tragedy, her attributes were the tragic mask, and also the club of Hercules.
5. *Terpsichore*—Whose attribute was the kithara (a harp with seven to eleven strings), the Muse of lyric poetry and of the dance.
6. *Erato*—The Muse of love poetry.
7. *Polyhymnia*—Often having been the Muse of heroic hymns, Polyhymnia became the Muse of mimic art. She is represented in the attitude of meditation, with a finger in her mouth.
8. *Urania*—The Muse of astronomy, and her attributes were a celestial globe and compass.
9. *Calliope*—Who, first in rank among her sisters, was considered in turn to be the Muse of epic poetry and eloquence (beautiful-voiced). Her attributes were the stylus and tablets.

The Muses often frequented Olympus, where they added gaiety to the feasts of the immortals with their singing. The Muses preferred to dwell on Helicon, a high mountain in Boeotia whose wooded slopes were covered with fragrant plants which had the property of depriving snakes of their venom. Here, two main springs caused an agreeable freshness, the Aganippe and Hippocrene, which gushed forth under the hoofs of Pegasus. Both had the virtue of conferring poetic inspiration on those who drank their waters.

The Muses also liked to visit Parnassus, in Phocis, where they shared the company of Apollo. There the fountain of Castalian water gave poetic inspiration. The Muses were closely connected with the cult of Apollo and, as well as being patrons of poetry, they were guardians of the oracle of Delphi.

Like all goddesses the Muses were easily offended and harshly punished anyone who dared to compete with them. Pierus, King of Emathia in Macedonia, had nine daughters, the Pierides, who dared to challenge the Muses for a prize of poetry. They were changed into magpies by Apollo, and the Muses took over their name.

Originally the Muses were represented as virgins of the strictest chastity. Later all the Muses became less shy, and numerous love affairs were attributed to them.

OCEANUS

Lord of the freshwater streams which flow round the world.

His companion was Tethys and between them they brought forth all the rivers and streams. They also bore the light-stepping Oceanides who were three thousand in number. Among these were Clymene, Callirrhoe, Clytia, Perseis, Europa, Asia and Styx, who was the most eminent of them all.

Oceanus is not to be confused with the sea which is salt water.

ODYSSEUS (ULYSSES) (Plate 44)

Son of Laertes and Anticlea. Married to Penelope who had one son, Telemachus.

Odysseus had been one of the heroes who hid in the wooden horse which had been the means of the Greeks' entry into Troy, when they destroyed the city. After the fall of Troy, Odysseus was free to return to Ithaca with all his men, but the gods were so angry that they decided to punish the victors for their brutality.

Under Odysseus's command twelve vessels sailed from Troy. But the gods had planned many adventures which were as follows:

1. The Land of the Lotophages (Lotus-Eaters)

Once into the open sea Poseidon brewed up a hurricane which carried their ships to Libya, the land of the Lotus-Eaters. Their ships were in a very bad state of repair and needed many days' work on sails and masts. Libya was a strange country to Odysseus, so he sent scouts to spy out the land and its people. The three spies had a wonderful time, and were away so long that Odysseus had to go in search of them. Then the secret was discovered: the land of the Lotus-Eaters was a snare; the fruit of the lotus trees was the people's food; the juice was a nectar so beguiling that those who tasted it lost all wish for anything but to remain in the land. Odysseus ordered the men who had accompanied him to find the scouts, but on no account to eat. When they found the scouts they bound them and carried them back to their ships and sailed away. The spies soon recovered and were grateful for their rescue.

2. Odysseus and Polyphemus

After many days the ships sailed to within sight of the land of the Cyclops. Each giant had only one eye, placed in the centre of his forehead. Odysseus realised the danger of these strange giants. He decided to anchor eleven of his ships off a little island near by and sail only his own ship in case the giants panicked. With one ship and his friendly manner he hoped to obtain food.

When Odysseus reached the shore he saw that the land was rich in pasture, and cattle, goats and sheep roamed the fields. So he ran his ship ashore and with only twelve men he set out to find the owners of this land. Odysseus noticed a huge cave and decided to explore it. Inside there was an abundance of food but no owner, so they decided to await his return. Soon goats and sheep ran into the cave followed by a Cyclops who, to their alarm, closed the mouth of the cave with an enormous rock.

Polyphemus was the strongest and cruellest of the Cyclops. He lit the fire and soon its light revealed the thirteen men. 'Who are you? What do you want?' cried Polyphemus. His voice was so loud that it put the fear of death into them. It was some time before the great Odysseus could even speak, and then he answered the giant. 'My name is "No-man" and we have just come from the fields of Troy. Our ship was driven off its course and we were ship-wrecked on the coast of this island. We have come here for food and a place to stay until we can build another ship.' Odysseus misled Polyphemus in case he might seize their ship.

Odysseus's judgement of Polyphemus was right for he refused them food, ate his own meal and went to sleep, knowing full well that they would not harm him while he slept because Odysseus and all his men would not be able to remove the rock from the cave's entrance. Odysseus realised their predicament, so he devised a plan to escape. When Polyphemus arose he grabbed two of Odysseus's men and ate them for breakfast, he then allowed his flocks to leave and followed them. Once more he sealed up the opening.

Odysseus and his men who had survived, sat and awaited the return of the giant. All were in fear. They decided to explore the cave and in doing so came across the giant's club. This they fashioned into a spear, hardening the point in the fire and then they hid it for later use in Odysseus's plan, which they would carry out that night.

In the evening Polyphemus returned, letting his flocks in first while he stood guard, and then closing the cave with the rock once again. He sat down and made the fire for cooking his evening meal. Suddenly he snatched up two of the Greeks and killed them, to the dismay of the others. However, they had great faith in Odysseus's scheme.

Odysseus had a large pouch of wine which was very strong, and when the giant had eaten his fill, approached him with a cup filled with wine. Polyphemus had never tasted such wine and craved for more. 'No-Man', he shouted, 'give me more wine'. Odysseus did so and soon Polyphemus had drunk all of it and fell asleep. This was the moment that Odysseus had been waiting for. He and his men took the club they had fashioned into a spear and pierced the solitary eye of Polyphemus.

Polyphemus screamed and shouted so loudly that other Cyclops came to the cave to find out what was happening. They asked Polyphemus what was he screaming for and he replied 'No-Man hurts me! No-Man hurts me!' and he screamed in terror. The other Cyclops were confused and decided to leave Polyphemus to his mad outbreak. All night Polyphemus wandered the cave in agony and hate, trying to grab the men who had caused his misery. Soon, exhausted, he went to sleep.

In the morning Polyphemus decided to roll the rock away only sufficiently wide enough for one sheep or goat to pass through. By this method he hoped to keep trapped the men who had blinded his only eye. When Odysseus saw this he whispered to his companions to cling to the underneath of the sheep. One by one they passed out of the cave as Polyphemus ran his hand along the back of each sheep.

Soon Odysseus and his men were aboard their ship with a few sheep. After they had rowed away from the shore Odysseus decided to call out to Polyphemus whom he saw wandering about the shore, and taunt him for his inhospitality, revealing at the same time the real name of the man who put out his eye. Polyphemus was furious and started to throw great rocks in the direction of the voice of Odysseus. The Greeks had to move fast as the rocks fell too near for comfort.

3. The Winds of Aeolus

In due course, the Greeks came to the Aeolian Islands where Aeolus, King of the Winds, held sway. Odysseus and his men were treated kindly, and stayed for some time as the King's guests. The King wanted to listen to the stories they had to tell of the siege of Troy.

When Odysseus departed King Aeolus gave him a leather bag which contained and confined all adverse winds. Odysseus was told to hang this by the wheel of the ship and in nine days their ship would sight Ithaca. Tired after many nights awake, Odysseus decided to sleep. While he slept his companions, thinking that the leather bag contained something wonderful, opened it, and in doing so let out all the 'contrary' winds. Instantly a hurricane blew which took them back to Aeolus.

Odysseus went back to King Aeolus's palace where the King was feasting, and instead of the fine welcome they had received before, the King was angry with them for having opened the bag of wind. Besides, the gods were also angry with Odysseus for his treatment of Polyphemus who was the son of Poseidon, King of the Seas.

Odysseus and his men went back to their ships and sailed away. Poseidon decided to sweep them through raging seas for six days. Then they reached the island of the Lamus, who were giant cannibals. Luckily for Odysseus he did not go ashore, for all those who did so were taken prisoner. The giants sneaked up on the boats in the bay and hurled huge lumps of rock at the boats riding at anchor. Odysseus slashed the cables holding his boat and called upon his men to row strongly. Only a few Greeks escaped from the giant cannibals of Lamus.

4. The Island of Circe (Aeaea)

Once again the high winds and rough seas carried them to their next destination, the island of Circe, the sorceress.

Odysseus decided not to take any more chances. He divided his men into five groups, one to guard the ships, another under Eurylochus to explore the island. When Eurylochus came within sight of Circe's palace he heard sweet, charming music. The animals which roamed the area were tamed by the soothing sounds. Then Circe appeared and invited them into her palace. She was a beautiful woman with a soft and gentle voice. Eurylochus refused the invitation and warned his men to do so, but they were famished and on seeing the rich feast which was prepared fell upon it, without thought of danger. Eurylochus pretended to leave but hid to see if all was well. The food and wine had been drugged, and suddenly Circe waved her wand and the Greeks were turned into hogs! Eurylochus was astonished and rushed away to tell Odysseus.

Odysseus, enraged, rushed to the palace to confront Circe. He had not travelled very far when he was met by Hermes, who gave him a herb called Moly. This herb was an antidote to the poison Circe would put into his food. Odysseus was very grateful to Hermes and once again moved quickly to the palace, now having no fear of Circe, her poison or her charm.

The enchantress was pleased to see Odysseus and spread food and wine before him. Each and every particle held her drug. Odysseus drank and ate his fill, Circe then rose and waved her wand but Odysseus did not turn into a hog. Circe stared at Odysseus, wondering who this man could be, upon whom her drugs had no effect.

Odysseus seized his sword and rushed towards Circe, who crouched in terror and wept. Odysseus then demanded the release of his men. Circe was so amazed that she fell in love with him and restored the hogs once more to men.

They all decided to stay on the island and rejoice in the magic palace of Circe. Odysseus, although he loved Circe, began to think again of Ithaca and after some time he persuaded her to let them go. But she warned them: 'The gods have many things in store for you before you reach your native land.'

5. *The Sirens' Songs*

Odysseus was then told to set his sails and the winds would take him to the Underworld where Tiresias, the blind soothsayer, would foretell his future. When Odysseus had reached the spot Circe had mentioned, he dug a trench and offered sacrifices to the spirits.

Tiresias warned Odysseus that because of his treatment of Polyphemus he would suffer many more trials before he reached Ithaca. She warned him and his men how to protect themselves from many things including the Sirens' songs which lured many mariners to their death.

Odysseus took the wax that he had been given by Circe and filled his men's ears with it and they set sail. When the island of the Sirens was near he ordered his men to bind him to the mast, so that he could not get free for he wanted to hear the Sirens' songs. When he heard, Odysseus was seized with frenzy and struggled to be free. His men, frightened he might get free added more bonds. After they had passed, they untied Odysseus who, by that time, was exhausted after the ordeal. He rested in preparation for the next trial.

6. *Scylla and Charybdis*

Odysseus did not tell his men that they would have to pass between the two dreaded rocks of Scylla and Charybdis which were so close together that disaster awaited the ships which sought passage. On Scylla was a monster of the same name, who had six mouths, twelve feet and barked like a dog; while opposite, under the Charybdis, was a whirlpool which opened three times a day and swallowed the ocean waters.

Odysseus steered his men away from the whirlpool and all seemed well. But this was not to be, for Scylla suddenly swooped and reached out her long neck with six heads and seized half a dozen Greeks before Odysseus, with his shield and spear, could strike. The rest, so terror-stricken at the fate of their companions, pulled frantically and were out of danger before the monster could strike again. Soon the current swept them to Trinacria.

7. *Odysseus and the Cattle of Apollo*

When Odysseus's ships neared the island of Trinacria he remembered the words of Tiresias the soothsayer: 'Do not land there because it is the island of the Sun God, Apollo. The herds of cattle are sacred and you may be tempted to kill one. If you do, Apollo's wrath will descend upon you.' Odysseus warned his men of this and ordered them to sail on, but they were so tired that they said they only wanted to rest and they could go no further. It was useless to argue, but once again Odysseus warned them of the danger involved if they slaughtered the cattle. The men vowed to Odysseus that they would obey him.

For a week they stayed and rested on the island and replenished their stocks of food with fish and wild fowl. By this time Odysseus had told his men that they would soon set sail. Some of the Greeks were hungry for the meat of the beautiful cattle of Apollo and while Odysseus was away exploring, Eurylochus killed some of the sacred beasts. When Odysseus returned he was filled with remorse and wrath, but his men were not concerned. They all feasted and ignored Odysseus, they were even angry when he refused to join them.

For six days the men feasted and for six days a storm raged at sea. Lampetia, the guardian of the cattle, had told Apollo what had taken, place, and therefore, he wanted to let the Greeks have their fill before he punished them. On the seventh day the sea was calm, so Odysseus got his men aboard their ships and set sail hoping that Apollo had not yet learnt of their evil doings.

The calm was deceptive and when out of sight of land, a gale and huge mountainous waves engulfed them. The other ships capsized and one by one all but Odysseus was washed overboard and drowned.

Odysseus was alone and at the mercy of the wind and sea. His ship was being driven back to the dreaded place where Scylla lurked and Charybdis roared. No effort could keep him from the whirlpool. The vessel was caught by the swirl and started to go round and round getting nearer and nearer to the centre. Odysseus looked up and saw a fig tree jutting out from the island and with a mighty bound sprang up and caught it. As he hung on he looked down and saw his ship sucked down. He knew that after a certain time the whirlpool must disgorge the ship and become calm again. After several hours this happened and the vessel, a pitiful sight, appeared. Gradually it was once again beneath him. He let go his hold on the fig tree and leaped aboard. The waters were now drawing away from the Charybdis and fortunately Odysseus managed to row out of Scylla's way. For nine days he rowed and at last he reached the island of Ogygia, where lived the sea nymph named Calypso. As he reached the island Odysseus's ship broke up and he just managed to swim ashore, where he collapsed exhausted. Calypso nursed him to health and he remained with her for eight years. Odysseus hoped that one day a ship would land and take him to Ithaca.

8. *Odysseus's Homeward Voyage*
In Ithaca, treacherous friends were plotting to kill Odysseus's son, Telemachus, who had gone to Pylos in search of his father. Athene, the Goddess of Wisdom, had always watched over Odysseus and had urged Zeus to let the hero go back to his home. At last Zeus agreed, because Odysseus had been punished enough. Hermes was sent to Calypso to command her to instruct Odysseus to make a raft and set sail for home. Calypso loved Odysseus and was loath to give such instructions but she knew it was useless to disobey the gods. So Odysseus made a raft with a small sail and, assured of Calypso's instructions, put food and drink aboard and set sail. His troubles were not yet over, for Poseidon once again decided to punish Odysseus, and set great waves upon his tiny craft. This time Lencothea the sea nymph was sent to his rescue. 'Strip and plunge into the waves', she said, 'and put this scarf around your chest then you will not drown.' As Odysseus jumped into the sea the raft capsized, so he started swimming and for three days he swam until he reached the island of Phaeacia, where he made his way ashore. For all of three days Odysseus was held up in safety by the magic scarf and when he landed he was told to cast the scarf into the sea. He watched it being swallowed up by the receding tide. At last he came to a small forest where he covered himself with leaves and lay down to sleep, completely exhausted by the ordeal. While Odysseus slept, Athena went to the Court of Alcinous, King of the Phaeacia, and told his daughter Nausicaa to go down to the sea to wash her robes. The happy princess called her servants together and went down to the shore. Near where they washed, Odysseus slept.

The noise of the maidens awakened him, so he covered himself with vine leaves and approached them. Nausicaa welcomed Odysseus and after providing him with clothes, told him the way to the palace. Nausicaa left, and Odysseus started on his way to the palace. Hermes swathed a veil about him to make him invisible. When he was within the palace he threw himself at the feet of the Queen and paid homage. Soon he was seated at the King's table next to Laodamas, feasting in gay company.

Odysseus composed himself and told of his adventures, from the day he set sail from Ithaca to Troy and when he had finished the King and all his courtiers were moved with compassion. King Alcinous promised Odysseus all the assistance he could to enable him to reach Ithaca, and fitted out a vessel with treasures, provided a crew, and the next day Odysseus, under the watchful eye of Athene, set sail.

At last the ship reached Ithaca but Odysseus was asleep. The sailors ran their vessel ashore and after emptying the riches bore Odysseus to land still asleep on a couch. Poseidon, still angry, took vengeance on the men of Alcinous and wrecked the ship against the rock near the harbour of Phaeacia on the return voyage.

Ithaca

When Odysseus awoke from his sleep Athene appeared before him. She told him that he was in Ithaca. He should hide his treasures and she would turn him into a beggar. Once the treasure was hidden, Athene touched Odysseus. His hair turned white and his skin shrivelled —he became an old man that no one would recognise.

Odysseus decided to visit his swineherd Eumaeus, to find out how things stood at the court of Ithaca. Eumaeus was warm and friendly towards him and in conversation he found that most people of Ithaca believed Odysseus to be dead, and that a large number of suitors were pressing Odysseus's wife Penelope to choose a second husband. She, however, refused to do so.

Meanwhile, Telemachus, who had been to Sparta in search of information about his father, had been urged by Athene to return to Ithaca. Under her guidance he managed to foil his mother's suitors who had sent men to ambush him. Athene told Telemachus to go to the swineherd Eumaeus to ask him to inform his mother Penelope that he was safe. This he did, and when the swineherd had left, Odysseus and Telemachus met and conversed. Athene appeared before them. Then she touched Odysseus who was transformed from a weak beggar into his former self. Telemachus was amazed and wept when Odysseus cried out 'My son! I am your father'. Together they rejoiced. After a long conversation they planned a way to foil the suitors and plotters. For Odysseus to return to the palace as a beggar was the first stage of their plan.

Penelope's Web (Tapestry)

When Odysseus the beggar man arrived at the palace, only his old ailing hound Argu recognised him and was so overjoyed that he fell dead at his feet. The beggar was then brought to Penelope, who questioned him lest he should have any news of her husband. So effective was his disguise that Penelope did not recognise him.

For years Penelope had put off her suitors who had lived in the palace every day eating her best meats and foods. She told them that she would make her choice when she had finished the tapestry she was weaving. For three years little progress was made as she unpicked every night what she wove during the day, and when one of the suitors discovered this he related it to the others and they were all very angry.

Odysseus was very troubled when he saw the trials that Penelope had to endure. Although the suitors seemed friendly, they had tried to kill Telemachus because he became a hindrance to their plans. All were treacherous and greedy. He told Penelope that as only Odysseus could bend Odysseus's bow, she should make a new condition which would give her extra time, for he had heard that Odysseus was still alive, well and soon to be home. Penelope then proclaimed a new condition of marriage. 'To the man who can bend Odysseus's bow and drive an arrow through all twelve rings on this table—to that man I will give myself.'

So the contest began: one after another tried but all in vain. While the contest proceeded Odysseus revealed himself to the swineherd and his old maid who were overjoyed to see him. He told them of his plan, that all weapons should be carefully removed to avoid suspicion, and that all the doors be bolted.

When Odysseus asked if he could bend the bow, all the suitors laughed, but when he drew it full out and sped an arrow through all twelve rings there was an instant uproar. The suitors drew their swords, Odysseus gave a sign to Telemachus, then Athene appeared disguised as Mentor. With a touch she changed the beggar revealing Odysseus. The fight was fierce and bloody and all the suitors fell. When the fight was over Penelope, who was warned to stay in her bedroom, was told the news. When Odysseus came before her she was afraid to look upon him and could not believe that at last he was home. Then he disclosed to Penelope a secret that only the two of them knew, which was how he built the bridal chamber, she thus recognised him, and they lived to a great age in happiness together.

109

Plate 54. Oedipus and the Sphinx (See page 110) The Metropolitan Museum of Art,
Bequest by W. H. Herriman

OEDIPUS (*Plate* 54)
Son of Laius and Iocaste.

Laius received an oracle from Apollo at Delphi commanding him not to beget a son. Laius did not obey and so, when their son was born, his heels were pierced and he was left exposed to die on Mount Cithaeron. There he was found by Theban shepherds who gave him to their King, Polybus of Corinth, whose wife Merope was childless.

They called the baby Oedipus, which means 'swelled-foot' because of his pierced heels, and they brought him up as their own son. Oedipus did not know the terrible prophecy of Delphi, which was that he would kill his father and marry his mother.

One day on his return to Corinth, his chariot clashed with another at a crossroad. Blows followed and Oedipus killed the stranger, not knowing it was his father.

A sphinx had come to Thebes and asked travellers on the road to the city a riddle. Every time they failed to solve it she devoured one of them. Creon, brother of Queen Iocaste, promised his sister's hand in marriage to the man who could solve the riddle. The riddle was: 'Which is the animal that has four feet in the morning, two at midday and three in the evening?'

Oedipus decided to answer the riddle. He went to Thebes and confronted the sphinx. When she had asked the riddle he replied. 'Man, who in his infancy crawls on all fours, who walks upright on two feet in maturity, and in his old age supports himself with a stick.' The sphinx was vanquished and threw herself into the sea.

Thus without knowing it, Oedipus became King of Thebes and the husband of his mother, and the oracle was fulfilled.

Many years later an epidemic ravaged the land. Oedipus decided to consult the oracle at Delphi. The reply was that the epidemic would continue until the murderer of Laius was out of the country.

Oedipus decided to discover the murderer. His inquiries led him to the fact that he himself was guilty. When his wife and mother Iocaste found out, she hanged herself in anguish. Oedipus tore out his own eyes. Until his death, he wandered as a beggar, cared for by one of his devoted daughters who followed him from the city.

ORPHEUS (*Plate* 55)
Son of Apollo and Calliope.

When Orpheus played, rivers ceased to flow, beasts forgot their wildness; all nature was charmed and came before him to listen.

Orpheus was one of the Argonauts and played the lyre which put to sleep the fiery dragon who was guardian of the Golden Fleece. He also played it when the Argonauts passed the island of the Sirens,

Plate 55.   A fine Gobelin Tapestry depicting Apollo instructing Orpheus in the use
of the Lyre, circa 1680 (See page 110)

thereby saving his companions. For his music was so beautiful that
they did not hear the Sirens, whose song would have drawn them to
their deaths.

Orpheus married Eurydice whom he loved tenderly. One day she
was bitten by a snake and died. Orpheus decided to go to the Underworld and ask Pluto and Persephone if he might have her back. They
agreed, on one condition: that on his return to earth he would not
look back to see Eurydice, who would be following him. Approaching
the light he could no longer resist. She immediately became a shadow
and returned to Hades for ever. Orpheus died, heartbroken. There are
many versions of his death.

Plate 56.   A fine Paris Tapestry depicting the story of Pan and Syrinx, circa 1700
(See page 113)

PAN (*Plate* 56)
Son of Hermes and Dryope.
Greek God of the flocks.

Pan had the body of a man but his legs were the legs of a goat, and on his head he had a pair of goat's horns. He loved music and dancing and lived amongst the woods and glens. One day he caught sight of a wood nymph, a beautiful girl named Syrinx. Pan fell in love with her at first sight, but she was terrified of the strange god, and fled from him whenever she saw him.

One day Pan tried to speak to her but all was in vain—she just ran and became more frightened than ever. As she fled, his longing for her became greater, so he decided to chase her. He was gradually overtaking her when suddenly she found her way blocked by a stream. She raised her hands in despair. 'Help me' she cried to her father, the river god Ladon. As she cried out, she was drawn into the water and Pan saw her vanish. A moment later a clump of seven reeds sprang up from the same place. Pan knew that he would never see her again and was dreadfully unhappy, so he just sat on the bank staring at the reeds. He then decided to take a closer look, and while inspecting them his breath passed through the reeds, making sweet sounds. Pan was startled by the sudden music. Then he gathered the reeds and bound them together to make a pipe which he played so beautifully that it held everybody spellbound. Dying flowers revived and swung to and fro in the breeze, birds hushed their songs and butterflies hovered overhead and listened.

Pan called the instrument the Syrinx after the maiden he loved.

THE JUDGEMENT OF PARIS (*Plates* 44, 57 *and* 58)
The goddesses resented Aphrodite, and were determined to dispute the prize of beauty with her. The time came when Eros, who was infuriated by not being invited to Olympus, tossed a Golden Apple, inscribed with the words 'For the Fairest', into the hall where all the guests were gathered. Hera, Athene and Aphrodite each claimed it. To settle the affair, Zeus ordered them to submit the argument to the judgement of a mortal. Choice fell upon Paris, son of King Priam of Troy. Hermes then conducted the three goddesses to where Paris was tending his father's flocks on the slopes of Mount Ida. Paris tried to refuse, but had to submit to the will of Zeus.

One by one the three goddesses appeared before him and attempted to influence his decision by reinforcing the power of their charms with alluring promises. 'If you award me the prize', said Hera, 'I shall make you Lord over Asia.' Athene promised to see that the young shepherd was always victorious in battle. Aphrodite, who could offer

Plate 57. A fine Florentine Tapestry depicting Aphrodite holding the golden apple, attended by Eros, circa mid 16th Century (See Judgement of Paris, page 113)

neither sceptres nor victories, merely loosened the clasps by which her tunic was fastened and unknotted her girdle; then she promised to give Paris the most beautiful of mortal women. The verdict was then delivered and the shepherd awarded the coveted apple to Aphrodite. In this way Paris won possession of Helen, wife of Menelaus; but neither Hera nor Athene forgave him the wound to their pride, and avenged themselves cruelly by delivering his country, his family and his people to devastation and to making sure that he, too, fell beneath the blows of the Greeks at the battle of Troy.

Plate 58. Judgement of Paris (See page 113)   The Metropolitan Museum of Art, Roger Fund

Son of Zeus and Danae.

Acrisius, King of Argos, had a beautiful young daughter named Danae. He loved her very much and yet at the same time, he feared her because of the Oracle of Delphi which had declared 'his daughter's son would kill him'. Fearing the words of the oracle, King Acrisius decided to lock Danae up in a tower which had just one door and he kept the only key on his person.

Zeus fell in love with the beauty of Danae. He reached her in the guise of a 'shower of gold' and made her the mother of his son, Perseus. Acrisius decided to punish Danae but had not the heart to put her and the child to death. So he commanded his soldiers to take Danae and her son down to the harbour and there place them in a chest which should be cast out to sea.

Zeus, who sees all, protected Danae and Perseus by making them sleep whilst piloting the chest over heavy seas to a calm bay on the island of Seriphus. There Dictys, King Polydectes's brother, was fishing and seeing the chest he cast his net over it and brought it ashore. He was astonished when he opened it and found Danae and Perseus dozing. 'Who on earth put you both in here?' he asked. When Danae told him her story he volunteered to take them home and treat them as his children.

They lived in peace for many years and Perseus grew up to be strong and kind. He was loved by Gods and men alike. Danae grew more beautiful and when King Polydectes's wife died, he wished to marry Danae. Danae however rejected him. Polydectes was so angry that he ordered Danae to be brought to the palace as his slave. So infuriated was Perseus when he heard the King's orders that he went to the palace to kill the King, and had it not been for Dyctes he might well have done so. Perseus took his mother to the Temple of Athena, from where King Polydectes would not dare to take her away or touch her.

King Polydectes was embarrassed by the whole situation and thought of a plot to get Perseus out of his kingdom. He gave a great feast in honour of his forthcoming marriage to Hippodameia and invited Perseus. Perseus was so poor that he was unable to bring a gift, and when he was before King Polydectes he was ashamed and angry, so much so that he cried out 'I will bring you a gift greater than all those put together'. 'What can that be?' asked the King. Perseus retorted 'Medusa's head'. As Perseus left, the King was relieved to think that was the last he would see of him.

Perseus left the island of Seriphos and reached the abode of the Graeae. The Graeae were three hoary witches, Dino, Eyno and Pephredo, who were grey from birth and only had one tooth and one eye amongst all three of them; these they used in turn. Perseus stole their eye and tooth, and by this action forced them to tell him where the Gorgon Medusa lived. Perseus then persuaded them to lend him first, a magic wallet in which he could conceal the Gorgon's head to keep himself safe from its effect, and secondly, a dark helmet which rendered its wearer invisible.

Perseus then set off on his journey. That evening he was visited by Athena and Hermes. Athena gave Perseus her shield, for those who looked at the Gorgon Medusa were turned into stone. Athena told Perseus to look at Medusa only through the reflection in the shield, which shone like glass, and he would be safe. Hermes gave Perseus his winged sandals which enabled him to travel quickly.

Perseus's journey took him to the garden of the Hesperides where he was given his final instructions. The Hesperides did not want Perseus to get killed by the Medusa so they sent him to their uncle, Atlas. Atlas said to Perseus that he would tell him where to find Medusa, the Gorgon, if Perseus in turn would promise to bring Medusa's head so that Atlas might look upon it. He said that he felt old and weary and his burden seemed greater every year. and he wished to be turned to stone. Perseus promised that if he survived he would keep his part of the bargain.

Perseus arrived where Medusa lived, wearing his cap of darkness, his shield held high so that he could see all below him. He waited for Medusa to appear. When she did Perseus swooped down and with his sword cut off Medusa's head. He quickly placed it into the wallet that the Graeae had lent him so as to render its effect harmless, and flew up to the sky. When he looked back he beheld two events: first, from the bleeding head of Medusa sprang Pegasus and Chrysaor; secondly, he saw Medusa's two sisters, Euryale and Stheno, who were immortal, flying after him. They were able to do so by the trail and smell of Medusa's blood. However, the winged sandals of Hermes could not be overtaken.

The first thing that Perseus did was to keep his promise to Atlas. When he showed Atlas the head, the sky turned into rock and there beyond the garden of the Hesperides lay the Atlas Mountains.

On Perseus's return to the island of Seriphos he saw Andromeda chained to a rock. Perseus fell in love with her at first sight. Suddenly he saw a huge serpent appear. Realising the danger, he immediately went to battle. Perseus tried to kill the serpent but it was far too strong. So he showed the serpent Medusa's head and turned it into stone. Perseus freed Andromeda and her father, King Cepheus, who watched the whole event, was only too pleased to grant him Andromeda's hand in marriage.

Perseus then took Andromeda back with him to Seriphos, where

Plate 59. A fine Brussels Tapestry depicting the story of Pomona and Vertumnus, circa 1580 (See page 119)

he found that his mother was being ill-treated by King Polydectes. He asked the King for an audience, which he was granted, only because the King thought Perseus had failed. Standing before the King and his followers, Perseus pulled out Medusa's head and cried 'Behold the promised gift!' Instantly King Polydectes and his followers were turned into stone.

Perseus then gave to Athena the head of Medusa which she placed on her shield. He returned to Hermes the winged sandals and to the Graeae the magic wallet and the dark helmet.

Perseus then decided to return to Argos with his mother and wife. King Acrisius remembered what the oracle had said long ago and fled when he heard the news. But fate had ordained that one day while Perseus was throwing the discus during funeral games, one would strike Acrisius and kill him, which it did.

POMONA AND VERTUMNUS (*Plate* 59)

Pomona was a wood nymph. No other Latin wood nymph could tend a garden more skilfully than she, none was more devoted to the cultivation of fruit trees. Her garden was her passion. The only thing she was afraid of was being attacked by a wooer, so she fenced herself inside her orchards to prevent the men she shunned from reaching her.

Vertumnus (a Roman god of change) fell in love with her, but as with the other suitors he too was shunned. So he then disguised himself as a rough harvester, a vineyard worker, a soldier and as a fisherman. On each occasion he had the opportunity to see his love and to enjoy her beauty. One day he pretended to be an old woman. Leaning on a stick he entered the well-kept orchard, and admired Pomona's fruit. Pomona welcomed her, and the two became friends. Eventually 'the old woman' persuaded Pomona to share her couch with her, and Vertumnus revealed his true form.

POSEIDON (NEPTUNE) (*Plate* 60)

Son of Cronus and Rhea. Brother of Zeus.

The God of the Sea who created the horse. Known as 'Earth-Shaker', Poseidon was indeed the God of Earthquakes. His attribute was the trident, and the animal sacred to him the horse, symbol of the gushing springs, and also the bull.

He established himself in his abode in the depths of the Aegean Sea, where he had built for himself a magnificent palace. When he left his palace he would harness to his chariot swift steeds with golden manes. Clad in armour, he hurled his chariot across the waves, and around him would frolic sea monsters, and all sea life, to render homage. The sea would open before him as his chariot flew lightly across the waves. Poseidon is also depicted surrounded by sea life and nymphs, amidst wild tempest.

Poseidon succeeded in seducing Medusa in the very temple of Athene. Infuriated by this profanation, Athene turned Medusa's hair into snakes. When Perseus decapitated Medusa, the blood which fell from the wound gave birth to Chrysaor and the horse Pegasus.

Poseidon loved Theophane and to protect her from other suitors, carried her off to the isle of Crumissa. The suitors followed, so he

Plate 60.   A fine Paris Tapestry depicting Poseidon and Amphritrite, circa 1670
(See page 119)

turned her into a ewe, the suitors and inhabitants into sheep, and himself into a ram. Theophane gave birth to the famous ram with a Golden Fleece.

Euphemus, son of Europa and Poseidon, received from his father the power of walking on the water, and was the second pilot during the expedition of the Argonauts.

After the shipwreck of the Persian Fleet off Cape Artemision in 480 B.C. the god Poseidon was worshipped as Poseidon Soter (the Saviour), a title normally reserved for Zeus. This explains why he is so greatly venerated in Greece and especially in Athens. Athene and Poseidon quarrelled over possession of Attica. To affirm his rights, Poseidon struck the rock of the Acropolis with his trident and caused a spring of salt water to gush forth. Athene in her turn caused an olive tree to sprout there, a tree which was still to be seen in the time of Pericles, in spite of having been burned by the Persians. Zeus settled the dispute in favour of Athene.

Poseidon's wife was Amphitrite, who was in origin the feminine personification of the sea. She was the daughter of Oceanus. Poseidon met Amphitrite on the isle of Naxos. When he asked for her hand in marriage she refused and fled to Atlas. Poseidon sent a dolphin to look for her. The dolphin discovered Amphitrite and brought her back to Poseidon, and as a reward Poseidon placed him among the constellations.

Amphitrite is seen at Poseidon's side on the divine chariots drawn by Tritons blowing conch shells. In her hand she sometimes holds a trident. From the union of Poseidon and Amphitrite was born a son, Triton, and two daughters, Rhodes who gave her name to the island, and Benthesicyme who settled in Ethiopia. Poseidon had many loves and innumerable mistresses, but only once did Amphitrite show jealousy, and this was for Scylla who was a nymph of rare beauty. Enraged, Amphitrite threw magic herbs into the pool where Scylla used to bathe, and changed her into a frightful monster.

PROMETHEUS

Son of Iapetus and Clymene and brother of Atlas.

Zeus decided to punish Prometheus for two reasons. The first, because he refused to accept Pandora, the wife Zeus had chosen for him. The second, because Prometheus stole fire from Olympus and gave it to mankind.

When Zeus observed the glowing fires in the dwellings of man, he ordered Hermes to take Prometheus to a rock on Mount Caucasus. On this rock Hephaestus chained Prometheus, where a vulture (or eagle) fed daily on his liver, for it grew again every night. Some mythologists say Prometheus suffered for thirty years; others, thirty thousand years. Prometheus was finally freed by Hercules who shot the predatory bird when it arrived on the mountain. This happened after his eleventh labour.

When freed Prometheus taught man to tame horses; the use of plants and their medicinal power; the use of clay and the cultivation of the ground. Later Prometheus joined the gods on Olympus.

PYGMALION (Plate 61)

In Amathus, Cyprus, there lived a sculptor named Pygmalion, who shunned all women, yet fervently venerated Aphrodite.

One day he started work on a marble statue of a woman, which turned out to be of such extraordinary beauty that he fell in love with it. Aphrodite took pity on him, and one day as he held the statue in his arms the marble suddenly moved and was miraculously alive.

Plate 61. Pygmalion (See page 121) The Metropolitan Museum of Art

Plate 62. A fine Paris Tapestry depicting the story of Pyramus and Thisbe, circa 1700
(See page 123)

PYRAMUS AND THISBE (*Plate* 62)

Forbidden by their parents to see each other, though they lived in adjoining houses, Pyramus and Thisbe held conversation and confessed their love through a chink in the wall which separated their homes. They agreed to run away and meet at the tomb of Numus under a white mulberry tree outside the city walls.

Thisbe arrived first, but was frightened away from the meeting place by a lioness; in her flight Thisbe dropped her veil which the lioness besmeared with blood. When Pyramus arrived, he found the bloody veil and concluded that Thisbe had been torn to pieces by wild beasts; in despair he killed himself with his sword. Thisbe returned, found her lover dead, took his sword and stabbed herself. Their blood soaked the ground under the tree, causing the white mulberry to turn purple.

Rhea Silvia was a vestal virgin. She was fetching water from a sacred grove when she was visited by the god Mars. She later bore him twins. Rhea Silvia's uncle, Amulius, was responsible for her, and he commanded that the children be drowned in the Tiber. However, the servants of Amulius laid them in a basket and floated it carefully downstream. The Tiber was at that time in flood, and the twins in the basket drifted and then lodged under a fig tree. It was under that tree that Romulus and Remus were suckled by a she-wolf. Later they were found by the shepherd Faustulus who cared for them.

When they were eighteen years old on 21 April, they founded Rome. During the building of the city, the twins fought each other and Remus was killed.

The Rape of the Sabine Women

The settlement prospered and Romulus gave protection to all strangers. A great problem arose because there were no women. Therefore men were sent out to neighbouring settlements to arrange marriages, but to no avail. Romulus decided to resort to a ruse, and he invited all the neighbouring settlements to games in honour of Consus, to be held during the Festival of Consualia. The invitation was accepted and the Sabini came in particularly large numbers, curious to inspect the new city. In the course of the games, the young men of Rome abducted all the maidens.

The persuasion and affection of those who were their new husbands caused the women to stay. The Sabine families prepared for war and their King, Acron, marched on Rome, and it was there that Romulus, in single combat, killed him, and dedicated the dead king's armour to Jupiter (Spolia Optima). It was the first triumph in Roman history.

SELENE (LUNA)

Daughter of Theia and Hyperion.

Selene represented the fair-faced moon, she was mild and gentle, and rode in a chariot drawn by two snow-white cows, or sometimes by mules. Over her head flies her veil in a wide crescent or else she wears a crown of rays and carries a torch. Every evening before she started on her course Selene bathed in the tide of Oceanus.

It is said that Selene had a beneficial influence on life on earth, as farmers still watch the phases of the moon to perform their various tasks at the right season. It is said that honey should only be taken from the bees during a full moon.

Plate 63. A Royal Brussels Tapestry depicting one of the seven virtues 'Hope', circa 1650. Hope is a boat drawn by two chained slaves (See page 126)

SEMELE AND ZEUS

The daughter of Cadmus was loved by Zeus many times, and Hera's jealousy was terrible when she learned of the relationship between Zeus and this mortal girl. So Hera visited Semele in disguise and suggested that she ask her lover to appear before her in all the brilliance of his majesty. Zeus tried in vain to dissuade Semele from making unreasonable demands, but Semele insisted. The god gave in and visited her in his chariot of glory, surrounded by lightning and thunder. The sight of the great god in all his dazzling splendour was too much for mortal eyes and Semele perished, consumed by celestial flames. Zeus gathered up the child she bore in her womb, and enclosed it in his own thigh until the day of its birth: it was to be Dionysus.

THE SEVEN VIRTUES (*Plate* 63)

(Latin names in parentheses)
1. Prudence   (Prvdenza)
2. Justice   (Ivstitia)
3. Faith   (Fides)
4. Charity   (Charitas)
5. Hope   (Spes)
6. Fortitude   (Fortitvdo)
7. Temperance   (Temperanza)

They are depicted as follows:
1. Prudence holds a snake and a mirror showing two faces; Solon sits before her.
2. Justice holds scales and a sword; before her sits the Emperor Trajan.
3. Faith holds a chalice and a cross; St. Peter sits before her.
4. Charity holds a small child in one hand and a flame or heart in the other; St. John the Divine sits before her.
5. Hope prays; before her sits St. James the Greater.
6. Fortitude holds a column to indicate Samson's destruction of the Philistine temple; Samson sits before her.
7. Temperance holds two vases; Scipio Africanus sits at her feet.

TEIRESIAS

Teiresias was the greatest of all prophets. He was descended from the Spartae, and he lived to a great age, which, it is said, spanned seven generations.

There are two main stories about his blindness.

The first story is that Athena caught him watching her bathe in the Fountain of Hippocrene (as Acteon surprised Artemis) and she made him blind. To compensate Teiresias for his blindness Zeus bestowed on him the gift of prophecy and long life.

The second story is that Zeus and Hera argued about who derived more pleasure from sex, a man or a woman. So they consulted Teiresias who had been both and who could speak from experience, for when he had been a woman he had married. Teiresias said a woman received more pleasure from the physical aspect of love than did the man. Hera was so furious, because this statement would only encourage Zeus in his infidelities, that she blinded Teiresias.

Teiresias (man/woman/man)

The story of his change of sex is that he saw two snakes mating, killed the female, and immediately became a woman. After seven years as a woman, he again saw two snakes mating, killed the male, and thus became a man again.

Teiresias's prophecies were numerous and he was mentioned by most of the ancient writers. Six other prophets or soothsayers were: Amphiasans, Colchas, Cassandra, Helenus, Melampur and Mopsus.

TELEMACHUS
Son of Odysseus and Penelope.

After twenty years of his father's absence, Telemachus decided to seek information from the courts of Menelaus and Nestor. When he returned to Ithaca, he learned that Penelope's many suitors had planned to murder him, but he avoided the trap, and with the help of Athena learned that his Father had arrived home two days before and was staying in the house of the swineherd Eumaeus. With the help of his father and others, he slew his mother's suitors.

THESEUS (Plate 64)
Theseus was the hero of Attica. His mother was Aethra and he was fathered by both King Aegeus and the god Poseidon. Theseus thus had two fathers by this double union, a mortal and a god.

King Aegeus and Queen Aethra lived in Delphi and after Theseus was born Aegeus was obliged to return to Athens. Before he left he placed his finest sword and his best sandals under a very heavy rock, with instructions that when Theseus was strong enough to lift the rock, he should join his father in Athens.

Theseus was brought up by his mother in Delphi and while he was still very young his mother gave a party for him. During this party Hercules, who was visiting his mother, decided to play a joke on the children. Hercules threw near their table the terrifying skin of the Nemean lion. All the children fled except Theseus who decided to attack the skin, thinking it was alive. From this action he established a reputation for bravery, and became Hercules' friend.

When Theseus was sixteen Aethra revealed to him the secret of his birth and showed him the huge rock under which his father had placed the sword and sandals. She also told him the instructions his father the King had given. It was not until his eighteenth birthday that Theseus was able to lift the rock. On that day he decided to journey to Athens, a strong and mighty warrior.

Theseus's Adventures on his Journey to Athens
1. Near Epidaurus Theseus killed a dangerous bandit Periphetes, son of Hephaestus. He took from him his terrible club.
2. In the forest of Isthmus Theseus inflicted on Sinis, son of Poseidon, the same torture which Sinis imposed on others, which was tearing them asunder by tying them to sprung pine-trees.

Plate 64. A fine Flemish 17th Century Tapestry depicting Theseus with King Lycomedes. The King pushes Theseus over the cliff (See page 127)

Plate 16. A section from a tapestry in Chichester Cathedral

Plate 17. A John Piper tapestry in Grocers' Hall

3. Theseus killed the wild sow of Crommyon, called Phaea.
4. On the slopes of Megaris Theseus dashed Sciron against a boulder. Sciron had forced travellers to wash his feet, and when they stooped to do so, he would kick them over the cliff into the sea where they were devoured by a monstrous turtle. When Sciron gained consciousness Theseus threw him to the turtle.
5. At Eleusis Theseus vanquished their King Cercyon who made all strangers wrestle with him. The King had defeated and killed all but Theseus.
6. Just past Eleusis the giant Polypemon, known as Procrustes, forced his victims to lie on a bed which he knew was too short for them, and then cut off whatever overlapped. Alternatively he would stretch them if by chance the bed proved too long. Theseus made him undergo the same treatment and then killed him.

After all these killings Theseus went to the banks of the Cephissus to purify himself before entering Athens.

Theseus at Athens

Theseus donned a white robe and arranged his long hair, for he would soon be at the gates of his father's palace. Upon his arrival he found a feast was being held and to his surprise he was invited in without being announced. King Aegeus had meanwhile married Medea who became instinctively jealous of Theseus although she did not know him; so much so, that she decided to poison him. Theseus became suspicious when he smelt a strange odour just as he was about to drink his wine. He threw his cup on the floor, stood up and drew his sword. His father recognised him by the weapon and shouted 'Theseus, my son!' He went and embraced him. While doing so they noticed a dog lying dead after tasting the wine that Theseus had thrown to the floor. King Aegeus drove Medea and her children away and shared his throne with his son, Theseus.

Adventures of Theseus from Athens

1. Theseus exterminated the Pallantids who were the nephews of Aegeus and had schemed to overthrow their uncle.

2. Theseus then went in search of the wild Marathon bull which was devastating Attica. He succeeded in capturing the beast, brought it back to Athens and sacrificed it to Apollo.

3. *Theseus and the Minotaur.* It was the third time that the ambassadors from Crete had come to collect seven virgins and seven young men. This was a penalty which had been imposed on Athens since the death of Androgeus who was killed by the Marathonian bull. Minos declared

war on Athens but peace was re-established on the conditions that every year these young people should be sent to Crete. When they arrived in Crete they were thrown as food to a monster called the Minotaur. The Minotaur had the body of a man and the head of a magnificent white bull, and was fed human flesh.

Theseus embarked with the victims with the intention of destroying the monster Minotaur. He told his father that if he was victorious the ship, when it returned to Athens, would carry a white sail; if he were vanquished the black sail would be retained. When Theseus arrived in Crete he told them he was the son of Poseidon. To test this boast King Minos tossed a golden ring into the sea and requested Theseus to bring it back. Theseus dived into the sea and returned, not only with the ring, but with a crown which Amphitrite (Goddess of the Sea and wife of Poseidon) had given him.

Ariadne, daughter of King Minos, fell in love with Theseus, and on condition that he would marry her, she gave him the clue with which he was to find his way out of the Labyrinth. The Labyrinth at Knossos was where the Minotaur was kept. Ariadne's clue was a ball of string, which Theseus tied to the entrance of the Labyrinth and kept hold of the string. When he found the Minotaur, he killed him and by means of the string found his way out again. Theseus then bored holes in the Cretan ships so that King Minos would not follow him and, taking Ariadne with him, sailed away with all the fourteen youngsters.

When Theseus, Ariadne and the young Athenians reached Naxos, Dionysus appeared and claimed Ariadne in the name of Zeus. So Theseus had to leave Ariadne and sail on to Athens. He was so sad at his loss that he forgot to change the black sail. King Aegeus was waiting at Poseidon's temple at Sounion looking out for the ship. When he saw the black sail of the ship, he believed Theseus dead and threw himself over the cliff into the sea.

Theseus became King of Athens and united his people into a single group and endowed them with wise institutions.

4. Theseus accompanied Hercules on his ninth labour which was to bring back the belt (or girdle) of Queen Hippolyta of the Amazons. On their arrival the Amazons at once took up arms and in the battle many were killed. Hercules captured Queen Hippolyta and took the belt, and would have killed the Queen but Theseus who had fallen in love with her for her bravery, asked Hercules to spare her life and give her hand in marriage. Theseus married Hippolyta and both were very happy. They had one son who they called Hippolytus.

After many years Hippolyta died and Theseus looked for a new wife. He chose Ariadne's sister Phaedra, the other daughter of King Minos, who was now very friendly and had great respect for Theseus.

5. Theseus still looked for adventure and decided to help his friend Peirithous to abduct Persephone from the Underworld. They succeeded in getting into Hades but it took Hercules to rescue Theseus. Peirithous was left sitting in the chair of forgetfulness held by serpents. This was Hades' punishment for his impudence.

On Theseus' return to Athens, Phaedra falsely accused his son Hippolytus of raping her. Theseus believed Phaedra's charges and called his father Poseidon to punish his son, which he did. (See *Hippolytus and Phaedra*, p. 91.) Phaedra was so sorrowful at Hippolytus's death that she hanged herself.

Sorely stricken by these tragedies, Theseus left Athens and retired to Skyros where he lived with King Lycomedes, who he believed to be his friend. But King Lycomedes was very jealous of his guest and the stories he had to tell. One day he treacherously pushed him over a cliff into the rocks and sea. The remains of Theseus were interred in Skyros.

Many years later King Cimon, ruler of Athens, brought from Skyros a gigantic skeleton, believed to be that of Theseus, which was laid with great solemnity in a specially built shrine called the Theseum.

ZEUS (*Plate* 65)
Zeus was son of Cronus and Rhea.

Zeus was the most powerful of all the Greek gods, Ruler of Heaven and Earth, Ruler of all other gods, and of all men. It is said that one day all the gods on Olympus tied a chain around Zeus and tried to dethrone him. Zeus pulled them to him, one by one, as a father would with little children playing tug-of-war. Such was his strength.

The Greeks respected Zeus for his protection of the weak, his justice, wisdom and power. They also understood his passions and infidelities, which rendered him more human and more easy to understand. Zeus is pictured as a mighty, bearded man, seated on his throne with an eagle at his side. In his left hand he holds a sceptre, in his right hand a thunderbolt.

Zeus married eight times, and his wives were:

1. Thymbris   who bore Pan
2. Metis   who bore Athene
3. Themis   who bore the Horae (Wisdom, Justice, Peace)
4. Demeter   who bore Persephone
5. Euryhome   who bore the Three Graces

Plate 65.   A fine Tapestry depicting Zeus and Hera (See pages 131 and 83)

6. Leto   who bore Apollo and Artemis
7. Mnemosyne   who bore the Nine Muses
8. Hera   who bore Hebe, Ilithyia, Ares and Hephaestus

The Infidelities of Zeus
Zeus changed himself into many forms to satisfy his passions. They are as follows: into—

1. a shower of gold   Danae
2. Satyr   Antiope
3. swan   Leda
4. white bull   Europa
5. flame of fire   Aegina
6. horse   Dia
7. bull   Demeter
8. cuckoo   Hera
9. Artemis   Callisto
10. Amphitryton   Alcmene

Other loves of Zeus were: Carme, Dione, Elara, Electra, Io, Maia, Protogemia, Semele, Styx, Taygeta. There were good reasons why his last wife, Hera, was considered to be the most jealous in mythology. There are many stories about Zeus, and his adventures of love, of which many parts have been used by Western writers and painters.

Philosophy

THALES (a Phoenician) 585 B.C
One of the Seven Sages, Thales was the First Sage of Athens.
'. . . Of all things that are, the most ancient is God, for he is uncreated.
. . . The most beautiful is the universe, for it is God's workmanship.
. . . The greatest is space for it holds all things.
. . . The swiftest is the mind for it speeds everywhere.
. . . The strongest, necessity, for it masters all.
. . . The wisest, time, for it brings everything to light.'

PLATO 422–347 B.C.
'. . . It is no wonder then that we talk thus and are pleased with our-
selves and think we are fine folk. For a dog appears the fairest of things
to a dog, an ox to an ox, an ass to an ass, and verily a pig to a pig.
. . . I consider whether it is the blood or air or fire with which we
think, or none of these things but the brain, which furnishes the senses
of hearing and sight and smell and from these arise memory and
opinion and from memory and opinion, when they have become
stable, in the same way knowledge arises.'

ALEXANDER AND DIOGENES BY THE BARREL (356–323 B.C.)
(*Plate* 66)
   Alexander: 'I am Alexander the Great. Who are you?'
   Diogenes: 'I am Diogenes the Cynic.'
   Alexander: 'Are you afraid of me?'
   Diogenes: 'Why? Are you a good or a bad thing?'
   Alexander: 'A good thing.'
   Diogenes: 'Who then is afraid of a good thing?'
   Then Alexander came close to Diogenes and said: 'Ask of me any
boon you wish.'
   Diogenes replied: 'Stand out of my light.'
   Alexander then stated: 'Had I not been Alexander, I should have
liked to be Diogenes.'

DIOGENES (404–323 B.C.)
The child One day he observed a child drinking out of his hands,
so he cast away his cup from his wallet with the words: 'A child has
beaten me in plainness of living.'
   He also threw away his bowl when, in a like manner, he saw the
child who had broken his plate taking up his lentils with the hollow
part of a morsel of bread.

Plate 66. A fine Mortlake Tapestry depicting Alexander and Diogenese, circa 1700 (See page 134)

Diogenes reasoned thus: 'All things belong to the gods. The wise are the friends of the gods, and friends hold things in common. Therefore, "All things belong to the wise".'

Education
1. Controlling grace to the young.   2. Consolation to the old.
3. Wealth to the poor.   4. An ornament to the rich.
Charity 'If you have already given to anyone else, give to me also: if not, begin with me.'
Disabled Should not apply to either the deaf or to the blind, but to those who have no wallet.
The fingers If you go with your middle finger stretched out, some will think you mad, but if it is the little finger, they will not think so.
Writing on the door A eunuch of bad character had inscribed on his door the words: 'Let nothing evil enter'.

'How', asked Diogenes, 'is the master of the house to get in?'
Officials Once Diogenes saw the officials of a temple leading away someone who had stolen a bowl belonging to the treasurers, and he said: 'The great thieves are leading away the little thief.'
Gold Asked why gold is pale, he said, 'Because it has so many thieves plotting against it.'
Death Asked whether he had any maid or boy to wait on him, Diogenes said 'No'. They then asked, 'If you should die, who then will carry you out for burial?' Diogenes replied, 'Whoever wants the house'.

Marriage   Asked what was the right time to marry, Diogenes replied 'For a young man, not yet; For an old man, never at all'.
Evil When someone declared that life is evil, Diogenes corrected him: 'Not life itself, but ill living'.
Begging Beg from a statue to get practice in being refused. When begging of a miserly man who was slow to respond, Diogenes said: 'My friend, it is for food that I am asking, not for funeral expenses'.

When begging from a bad-tempered man who said 'Yes, if you can persuade me', Diogenes replied: 'If I could have persuaded you, I would have persuaded you to hang yourself'.
Philosophy Asked what he had gained from philosophy, Diogenes replied: 'This at least, if nothing else—to be prepared for every fortune'.

To a man who said, 'You don't know anything', he replied: 'Even if I am a pretender to wisdom, that itself is philosophy'.
A father To one who despised his father: 'Are you not ashamed,' said Diogenes, 'to despise him to whom you owe it that you can so pride yourself?'
Life 'Why then do you live, if you do not care to live well?'
The child of a courtesan Seeing the child of a courtesan throwing stones at a crowd, Diogenes said, 'Take care you don't hit your father'.

Three Teniers' Tapestries

The three Teniers' Tapestries (*Plate* 67) are in the American National Bank and Trust Company of Chicago, U.S.A. They were purchased by Jack Franses of Franses of Piccadilly, 169 Piccadilly, London W.1., from Uppark, the family home of the late Sir Harry Fetherstonhaugh.

The History of Uppark

Much of the masonry in the basement of the existing house is fifteenth century work and there are other indications of an older building. The land on which it stands falls gently to the English south coast, and from the house one can glimpse the sea beyond Chichester and the Isle of Wight across the Solent twenty miles away.

It was not until about 1650 that the problem of pumping water to a considerable height was solved, and this event was intimately connected with Uppark. The first effective pump was invented by Sir Edward Ford, whose family had owned Uppark and the Manor of East Harting for two centuries. Wood, in his *Athenae Oxoniensis* describes the debt that Londoners owe to Sir Edward:

> Edward Ford of Uppark was a most ingenious mechanist and being encouraged by Oliver [Cromwell] and invited by the citizens of London in 1656, he raised the Thames water into all the highest streets of the city, ninety-three feet in four eight-inch pipes, to the wonder of all men, and the Honour of the Nation, with a rare engine of his own invention, done at his own charge and in one year's time. . . .

His ingenuity was not limited to the construction of water works: he tried his hand at other mechanical problems, and worked with successive political parties. Though he defended Arundel Castle unsuccessfully for Charles I, he escaped with a light fine and became First Lord of the Works under Cromwell, being confirmed in that office by Charles II at the Restoration—an impartial political record.

In his private life he was equally impartial, since, although he served two Kings, he married Sarah Ireton, who was the sister of General Ireton, the husband of Cromwell's daughter.

Uppark was partly rebuilt by William Talman. The exact date is not known; some accounts state that the year was 1685, and some 1690. It was undoubtedly a fine conception, but Lord Tankerville could hardly have built it had it not been for his grandfather's invention. The latter made it possible to bring to the house good water in pipes of lead and Sussex iron from St. Richard's Spring a mile away and some 350 feet below the summit of the Downs on which the mansion stands. The original water wheel is still to be seen in its small house beside the spring.

By 1751 Sir Matthew estimated that he had spent a further £16,615 at Uppark on buildings, furniture, pictures, furnishings, books and horses, including the collection made on his Continental tour between the years 1749 and 1751. By the last quarter of the eighteenth century Uppark became the centre of country life for the fashionable, and in 1785 Sir Harry Fetherstonhaugh was honoured by a visit from H.R.H. George III, the Duc de Chartres, the Duke of Queensbury, Lord Grosvenor, and others.

The Tapestry Room contains three seventeenth century Brussels tapestries, woven by the firm of Urbain and Daniel Leyniers after designs by Teniers. The subjects are 'Village Fete'; 'The Return from Harvest'; and 'The Vintage'. A Chippendale four-poster known as the Prince Regent's bed, which was covered in red damask and brought to Uppark by Sarah Lethieullier, is also in the room.

The Weavers

The weavers of the tapestries from designs by David Teniers II (1610–1690) were Urbain and Daniel Leyniers. The celebrated family of Leyniers had several Master Weavers during the seventeenth and eighteenth centuries. The earliest Urbain was born in Brussels in 1674, and when eleven years old became an apprentice in the workshops of his father Gaspard Leyniers who was a Master Dyer.

In 1700, Urbain was made a Master Weaver and for nineteen years was in partnership with Henri Reydams who had five looms in Brussels. When Henri Reydams died in 1719, Urbain Leyniers' brother Daniel filled his place and business developed rapidly. They bought genre cartoons from Jan Van Orley, and country scenes from Teniers. Their workmanship was the finest of the period. Tapestries attributed to them are as follows:
1. 'Hunting Scenes' in the Austrian State Collection.
2. Two Sets of the 'Story of Achilles'—one in the Palace of Liege, the other in the Royal collection of Vienna.
3. 'The History of Telemachus' in the State collection of Vienna.

Plate 68. A fine 18th Century Brussels Tapestry 'The Village Fete' (Kermesse) woven by Judocus de Vos, designed by David Teniers. Size 11' high × 14' wide

4. 'Peasant Life' in Wemyss Castle, Fife, Scotland.
5. 'Country Life' in Brahan Castle in Ross-shire, Scotland.
6. 'The Triumph of Mars' at Bowhill House, property of the Duke of Buccleuch.
7. A set of three: 'Village Fete' (De Kermis); 'The Return from Harvest' (Terugkeer Van De Oogst); 'The Vintage' (De Wijnoogst) at Up-park, Sussex. Now at the American National Bank and Trust Company of Chicago.

In 1728 Daniel Leyniers died and Urbain then brought his son into the business to help him. Urbain Leyniers retired in 1745 and died two years later.

The Tapestry Surround

The tapestry which surrounds the three Teniers which include the cartouches, was designed by the Bank's architects, and Jack Franses, of Franses of Piccadilly, and woven in 1972 by Robert Four of Aubusson, France.

David Teniers the Younger 1610–1690*

Juliaen Teniers, a linen draper, had two sons, both of whom were painters: Juliaen the Elder (1572–1615) and David (also known as the Elder) (1582–1649). The latter married Dymphna de Wilde (1608) and they had four sons and a daughter. The four sons were all painters, David the Younger (1610–1690), Juliaen the Younger (1616–1679), Theodor (1619–1697) and Abraham (1629–1670).

Plate 69. A fine Brussels Tapestry depicting 'The Grape Harvest' by David Teniers, circa 1720. Size 10′ high × 11′ wide

* Rye Art Gallery, Rye, Sussex.

Plate 70. 'The Fish Quay'. A fine 18th Century Brussels Teniers Tapestry by P. Van de Borcht.

1610   David Teniers the Younger born in Antwerp, baptised on 15 December.

He became a pupil of his father, and by tradition also of Peter Paul Rubens (1577–1640). But there is no firm evidence that he entered Rubens's studio, rather that he obtained advice and criticism from Rubens (Descamps, *La Vie des Peintres Flamands,* vol 11, p. 160). He was also influenced by his precocious friend Adriaen Brouwer (*circa* 1605–1638).

1629   He organised sales of paintings, his own and those of his father, to obtain the release of David the Elder from prison where the father was being penalised for a property fraud.

1633   Master of the Antwerp Guild of St. Luke.

1636   Visit to Dover to confer with van Immerseel, the Seville dealer, who ordered some paintings to be delivered to Antoon Cossiers, Teniers's agent in Antwerp.

1637   Married on 4 July, his bride being Anna Brueghel, the daughter of the painter Jan (Velvet) Brueghel. They were to have two sons and three daughters.

1638   The first son was born, and baptised on 10 July. He became a painter, David Teniers III (1638–1685).

1645   Doyen of the Antwerp Guild of St. Luke.

1647   Painted the signed and dated 'The Archduke Leopold-Wilhelm at a Village Fete' which has led some recorders to assert that he was appointed Court Painter to the Archduke in this year.

1649   Death of his father. Soon after, David the Younger left Antwerp, moving to Brussels and entering the service of Archduke Leopold-Wilhelm as Court Painter, Chamberlain and Curator of his gallery, where he subsequently made copies of the Italian paintings for 'Theatrum Pictorium'.

1650–5   Visited England to purchase pictures for Count Fuensaldana who is depicted as one of the figures in 'Archduke Leopold-Wilhelm in his Picture Gallery at Brussels' (Madrid).

1656   Death of his wife Anna (Brueghel); married Isabelle de Fren, daughter of Andre de Fren, Secretary of Conseil du Brabant.

1662   Bought the château at Perck der Drie Toren from J. B. Broekoven, Count of Bergeijck and his wife Helena Fourment, who had previously been married to Rubens. In this year David the Younger was one of the instigators of the establishment of the Antwerp Academy (founded 1663).

1672   Grandson was born. He became a painter, David Teniers IV (1672-1771).

1680   For many years David Teniers had sought to become ennobled but had been informed that any dealing in pictures had to be renounced as a condition. In this year patent of nobility was finally granted (Vermoelen, *Journal des Beaux Arts*, 1865, p. 10).

1683   Death of his second wife Isabelle (de Fren) who had led him into various extravagances, thus Teniers's later years were saddened by financial troubles and the children of the first marriage were in long conflict with those of the second, bringing ruinous actions which were not resolved until after Teniers's death.

1690   Death of David Teniers the Younger in Brussels on 25 April.

David Teniers was regarded as second only to Rubens. In 1970 The Hermitage Museum in Leningrad held an exhibition to mark the 350th Anniversary of Teniers's birth. It was Sir Joshua Reynolds who held that the works of Teniers are worthy of the greatest admiration, words which have not had the attention that they deserve. More than two thousand pictures are catalogued under his name in public or private collections.

Rubens and his studio closely embraced the influence of the Italian Renaissance. But the art of Teniers remained strongly rooted in Gothic tradition, and everyday life depicting people doing simple things in simple country surroundings. Herein lies the poetry of David Teniers the Younger.

Acknowledgements

My late father

Philippa, who helped me

Readers, Roy Macey, Philippa Franses, P. Nahum.

Many thanks to: Lord Milne, Marquis of Bute, John Piper, Jerry Harper, Archie Brennan, Whitworth Art Gallery, University of Manchester, Mrs. Meade-Fethstonehaugh, Ronald Lee, Cluny Museum, Paris, The Metropolitan Museum of Art, New York.

Photographs of the tapestries were kindly supplied by the following:

Christie Manson & Wood

Robert Four, Paris.

Jack Franses Ltd

Franses of Piccadilly

Perez

Sothebys

The Victoria and Albert Museum

The Vigo Sternberg Galleries

Bibliography

1. W. G. Thompson, *A History of Tapestry*.
2. W. G. Thompson, *Tapestry Weaving in England*.
3. George Leland Hunter, *Tapestries, Their History and Renaissance*.
4. Marillier, *English Tapestries of the Eighteenth Century*.
5. Moncrieff, *Classic Myth and Legend*.
6. J. E. Zimmerman, *Dictionary of Classical Mythology*.
7. Collins Larousse, *Collins Concise Encyclopedia of Greek and Roman Mythology*.
8. Larousse, *Mythology*.
9. Homer, *The Odyssey*.
10. Homer, *The Iliad*.
11. The Voyage of Argo, *Apollonius of Rhodes*.
12. Ovid, *Metamorphoses*.
13. Marcus Aurelius, *Meditations*.
14. Diogenese Laertius, Vols. I and II. Trans. R. D. Hicks. William Heinemann.
15. *My Beautiful Book of Legends*. Cassell & Co., Ltd.
16. The Rye Art Gallery, Rye, Sussex.
17. *The Golden Bough*. J. G. Frazer.
18. *The White Goddess*. Robert Graves.
19. *A Handbook of Greek Mythology*. H. J. Rose.
20. *Mythology*. Edith Hamilton.
21. *Greek Myths I*. Robert Graves.
22. *Painted Tapestry*. Julian Godon.

Signs and Symbols

A

Abducted	woman by man (Hades)	*Demeter (Persephone)*
	woman by man on chariot (Hades)	*Demeter (Persephone)*
	woman carried by man on horse (Agamemnon)	*Cassandra*
Anvil	man working at (Vulcan)	*Hephaestus*
Apples	one golden, inscribed	*Judgement of Paris*
	three golden (twelfth labour)	*Hercules*
	three golden, picked up in race	*Meleager, Atalanta and Melanion*
Argus	killing of	*Hermes*
	Having flute played to him	*Hermes*
Armour	-clad, and tall, crested helmet	*Ares*

B

Babies	suckled by she-wolf	*Romulus and Remus*
Bacchus	birth of	*Semele and Zeus*
Bag	being handed over by King Aeolus	*Odysseus*
Barrel	man inside, waving hand at general	*Diogenes*
Bath	murdered in (King Minos)	*Daedalus and Icarus*
	murdered in (King Agamemnon)	*Cassandra*
Bear	shooting arrow at	*Arcas and Callisto*
Bearded	blacksmith with hairy chest	*Hephaestus*
Bed	man lying on too short a bed	*Theseus*
	man lying on too long a bed	*Theseus*
	(secret) of Penelope	*Odysseus*
Beggar	in disguise, with boy or dog	*Odysseus*
Belt	being given to man by woman	*Hercules*
Bird's	feathers as arrows	*Hercules*
Blacksmith	at anvil	*Hephaestus*
Boar	being carried	*Hercules*
	-hunt, killing, or with boar's head	*Meleager, Atalanta and Melanion*
Book	maiden reading poetry	*Muse, Erato*
Bow	sacred to	*Apollo*
	drawn against bear	*Arcas and Callisto*
	sacred to	*Artemis*
	very big	*Odysseus*
Box	containing eternal youth	*Eros and Psyche*
	containing evils of the world (Pandora)	*Prometheus*
Boxer	being beaten and slain	*Hercules*
Boy	attacking lion (Nemean) skin	*Theseus*
Breast	one only (Amazon)	*Artemis*

146

Bull	white, with girl on back	*Europa and Zeus*
	metamorphosis	*Zeus and Demeter*
	two white, with fire in nostrils	*Jason*
	being carried	*Hercules*
	being led	*Hercules*
	sacred to	*Poseidon*
	captured by (Marathon bull)	*Theseus*
	lower half of body that of man (Minotaur)	*Theseus*
	being crowned with floral wreaths	*Europa and Zeus*
	carrying maiden out to sea	*Europa and Zeus*
Buskins	laced	*Artemis*

C

Carrying	man on back was Anchises, father of	*Aeneas*
Cattle	of Apollo being driven off by	*Hermes*
	red, driven off by	*Hercules*
	being stolen by the men of	*Odysseus*
Centaur	Chiron teaching	*Achilles*
Chained	girl to rock (Andromeda)	*Perseus*
Chalice	woman holds (Faith)	*Seven Virtues*
Changing	of people into animals, plants, rocks, streams, etc.	See *Metamorphosis*
Chariot	drawn by two horses	*Eos*
	in sea	*Amphitrite*
	in sea	*Poseidon*
Chariots	in collision	*Oedipus*
Chest	in sea, containing woman and child	*Perseus*
Child	holding two snakes	*Hercules*
	in woman's arms (Charity)	*Seven Virtues*
	drinking out of cupped hands	*Diogenes*
Chimaera	mythological beast	*Bellerophon*
Cicada	sacred to	*Apollo*
Clepsydra	with Clio	*The Muse*
Cloud	being held and caressed by man	*Ixion*
Club	of Hercules, held by Melpomene	*The Muse*
	large, held by	*Hercules*
	large, held by (taken from Periphetes)	*Theseus*
Cock	sacred to	*Apollo*
Coffer	with child inside (Underworld)	*Adonis*
Column	woman holds (Fortitude)	*Seven Virtues*
Comic	mask, held by Thalia	*The Muse*
Companions	three	*Three Graces*
Compass	held by Urania	*The Muse*
Conch shell	blown by	*Amphitrite*
Cone	-tipped staff, held by	*Dionysus*
Conical cap	worn by	*Ganymede*
Cow	white heifer by Hermes	*Io and Zeus*
Cows	two white, drawing chariot	*Selene*
Crescent moon	head-dress	*Artemis*
Cross	held by woman (Faith)	*Seven Virtues*
Crow	sacred to	*Apollo*
Crown	worn by	*Zeus*

Cuckoo	sacred to	*Hera*
Cup	of wine in hand	*Dionysus*
Cup-bearer	on Olympus	*Ganymede*
Cutting	down Golden Fleece	*Jason*
	off head of Medusa the Gorgon	*Perseus*

D

Dionysus	birth of	*Semele and Zeus*
	with maiden (Ariadne) on chariot at Naxos	*Theseus*
Discus	hitting man (Acrisius)	*Perseus*
Doe	(white) between two giants	*Artemis*
Dog	sacred to	*Artemis*
	with three heads (Cerberus)	*Hercules*
	with two heads (Orthus)	*Hercules*
	with three heads (Cerberus)	*Eros and Psyche*
	dead at beggar's feet	*Odysseus*
Dolphins	with Amphitrite	*Poseidon*
Dove	bird of love, sacred to	*Aphrodite*
Dragon	sleeping near Golden Fleece	*Jason*
Drowned	man by tower	*Hero and Leander*

E

Eagle	boy riding on or carried by	*Ganymede*
	at feet of crowned King	*Zeus*
	eating liver of man chained to rock	*Prometheus*
Ears	of an ass on King	*Midas*
Elephants	with army	*Hannibal/Scipio*
	with army	*Alexander*
Eros	winged boy	*Eros and Psyche*

F

Feet	washing of, by one man to another	*Theseus*
Finger	of maiden, in mouth (Polyhymnia)	*The Muse*
Fire	being made by rubbing sticks	*Hermes*
Flame	held by woman (Charity)	*Seven Virtues*
Flames	surrounding woman	*Hestia*
	burning woman (Creusa)	*Jason*
Flayed	man, by Apollo	*Marsyas*
Fleece	being cut down by	*Jason*
Flowers	Goddess of	*Chloris*
Flute	contest with Apollo and Muses	*Marsyas*
	played by Hermes to Argus	*Io and Zeus*
	played by Euterpe	*The Muse*
Fly	gadfly, stinging cattle	*Hercules*
	gadfly, stinging white cow or heifer	*Io and Zeus*
Flying	man with shield	*Perseus*
Flying horse	Pegasus, with woman on back	*Eos*
	Pegasus with man on back	*Bellerophon*
Fountain	man looking into	*Pyramus*

G

Giant	Polyphemus watches lovers (he is giant with one eye in middle of forehead)	*Acis and Galatea*
	blind, throws rocks at ships	*Odysseus*
	eating men in cave (Polyphemus)	*Odysseus*
	in cave	*Odysseus*
Girdle	being given to man	*Hercules*
	being given to shepherd (by Aphrodite)	*Judgement of Paris*
Globe	celestial, held by Urania	*The Muse*
Goats	goat's legs, body of man	*Pan*
Goddesses	three, being conducted by Hermes	*Judgement of Paris*
Gold	shower of, falling on woman in tower	*Danae and Zeus*
Golden	Fleece, being cut down by	*Jason*
	touch, all turns to gold	*Midas*
Grapes	in hand or on head	*Dionysus*

H

Half	man, half goat	*Pan*
Halo	about head	*Apollo*
Hammer	carried by, or used by	*Hephaestus*
Hanging	man from fig tree, over whirlpool	*Odysseus*
Harp	played by Terpsichore	*The Muse*
Hawk	sacred to	*Apollo*
Head	severed (Medusa the Gorgon)	*Perseus*
Heart	held by woman (Charity)	*Seven Virtues*
Heel	pierced	*Oedipus*
	pierced by arrow	*Achilles*
Heifer	white	*Io and Zeus*
Helmet	worn by woman	*Athene*
	with tall crest, worn by man	*Ares*
	of darkness, held by man	*Hades*
	winged, worn by man	*Hermes*
Hermes	with three maidens	*Judgement of Paris*
	playing flute to Argus	*Io and Zeus*
	tying a man to a wheel	*Ixion*
	selling Hercules to Omphale	*Hermes*
Hind	sacred to	*Artemis*
Horse	with woman Dia	*Zeus and Dia*
	wooden	*Troy*
	sacred to	*Poseidon*
Horse (Pegasus)	winged	*Pegasus*
	winged with woman on back	*Eos*
	winged with man on back	*Bellerophon*
Horses	black with golden reins, belonging to	*Hades*
	aboard ship, or being driven aboard	*Hercules*
Hounds	eating their master	*Actaeon*

J

Jar	with water flowing from it (held by man)	*Oceanus*
	with man sitting on its side	*Oceanus*
Javelin	used by, and sacred to	*Athene*
	piercing woman	*Cephalus and Procris*
	being thrown	*Cephalus and Procris*

K
Killing

(of Argus)	(Hermes plays flute)	*Hermes*
	(Hermes plays flute)	*Io and Zeus*
King (Aegeus)	throwing himself off cliff	*Theseus*
King (Aeolus)	handing over bag of winds, to	*Odysseus*
King		
(Lycomedes)	pushes man (Theseus) off cliff	*Theseus*
King (Minos)	murdered in bath	*Daedalus and Icarus*

L

Labyrinth	home of Minotaur	*Theseus*
Laurel	sacred to	*Apollo*
Leaves	worn by Hercules, signifying freedom	*Hercules*
Leaves (laurel)		
worn	signify freeing of Prometheus, by	*Hercules*
	worn by Odysseus on island of Phaeacia	*Odysseus*
Lion (Nemean)	man wrestling with	*Hercules*
Lioness	playing with veil besmirched with blood	*Pyramus and Thisbe*
Lion skin		
(Nemean)	on man's back	*Hercules*
	being attacked by boy	*Theseus*
Lyre	sacred to	*Apollo*
	being played to animals by	*Orpheus*
	being played aboard ship by Orpheus	*Jason*
	Apollo teaching	*Orpheus*

M

Man	half white, half black	*Hercules*
	tied to sprung pine trees	*Theseus*
	being pushed off cliff (by King Lycomedes)	*Theseus*
Mask	comic, in the hands of Thalis	*Muse*
	tragic, in the hands of Melpomene	*Muse*
	of darkness, in hands of	*Hades*
	of darkness, in hands of	*Perseus*
Mast	man tied to	*Odysseus*
Men	turned into stone (King and courtier)	*Perseus*
	turned into swine	*Odysseus*
Metamorphoses		
Acteon	into stag	*Acteon*
Arachne	spider	*Athene*
Arcas	constellation of Little Bear	*Callisto and Arcas*
Arethusa	a spring	*Arethusa and Alpheius*
Atalanta	lion with Melanion	*Atalanta and Melanion*
Callisto	a bear	*Callisto and Arcas*
	Great Bear constellation	*Callisto and Arcas*
Castalia	Castalian spring at Delphi	*Apollo*
Chione	a hawk	*Artemis*
Clyte	a sunflower	*Apollo*
Cycnus	a swan (with mother Thyria)	*Apollo*
Cyparissus	a cypress tree	*Apollo*

Daphne	a laurel tree	*Apollo*
Emathia's nine		
daughters	magpies	*Muses*
Hecuba	a female dog, bitch	*Cassandra*
Hyacinthus	a hyacinth	*Apollo*
Melanion	a lion, with Atalanta	*Atalanta and Melanion*
Men of		
Odysseus	swine	*Circe or Odysseus*
Narcissus	a narcissus	*Echo and Narcissus*
Niobe	a rock	*Artemis*
Shepherd	a wild olive tree	*Apulian shepherd*
Syrinx	seven reeds	*Pan and Syrinx*
Thyria	a swan (with son Cygnus)	*Apollo*
Zeus	a shower of gold	*Danae*
	a Satyr	*Antiope*
	a swan	*Leda*
	a white bull	*Europa*
	a bull	*Demeter*
	a flame	*Aegina*
	a horse	*Dia*
	a cuckoo	*Hera*
	a cloud	*Io*
Mirror	woman holding mirror (Prudence)	*Seven Virtues*
Monster	with nine heads (Hydra)	*Hercules*
	dog with three heads (Cerberus)	*Hercules*
	with six mouths (Charybdis)	*Odysseus*
	in sea	*Perseus*
	in garden, with many heads	*The Hesperides*
	serpent (Python) being killed by	*Artemis and Apollo*
	the Chimaera, being killed by	*Bellerophon*
	dog with three heads (Cerberus)	*Eros and Psyche*
	serpent of Lydia	*Hercules*
	of sea being rescued by (Hesione)	*Hercules*
	two-headed dog (Orthrus)	*Hercules*
	of sea, terrifying charioteer	*Hippolytus and Phaedra*
	half man, half bull (Minotaur)	*Theseus*
Moon	crescent headdress	*Artemis*
Mulberry	bearing half white and half purple fruit	*Pyramus and Thisbe*
Mules	two, drawing chariot of	*Selene*

N

Net	man and woman caught in net	*Ares and Aphrodite*
	laid as trap by Hephaestus	*Ares and Aphrodite*
	cast over trunk in sea	*Perseus*

O

Oak tree	sacred to, and its leaves crown of,	*Zeus*
Offering	the first was to Zeus by	*Hermes*
Olive tree	caused to sprout on Acropolis by	*Athene*
Orange	being carved on	*Acontius and Cydippe*
Orchard	two women, one young, one old	*Pomona and Vertumnus*

P

Palm tree	sacred to	*Apollo*
Pan	half man, half goat, playing Syrinx	*Pan and Syrinx*
Peacock	sacred to	*Hera*
Peacock		
feathers	(see *Io and Zeus*, p. 91)	*Hera*
	sacred to, and forming headdress of,	*Hera*
Pine cone	-tipped staff, held by	*Dionysus*
Pipes	played by half man half goat	*Pan*
Poetry book	read by Erato	*The Muse*
Pomegranate	held in left hand	*Hera*
	being eaten (in Underworld) by	*Persephone*
Pool	man gazing at his reflection	*Echo and Narcissus*
Potter's wheel	invented by, and sacred to	*Athene*
Praying		
woman	Hope	*Seven Virtues*

Q

Quiver	belonging to	*Apollo*
	belonging to	*Artemis*
	belonging to	*Adonis*

R

Race	and man dropping golden apples which are being picked up by woman	*Atalanta and Melanion*
Raft	on rough seas, man on raft	*Odysseus*
Rape	of Sabine women	*Romulus and Remus*
Reading	a book of poetry (Erato)	*The Muse*
Reflection	of himself in pool	*Echo and Narcissus*
Rescue	of maiden (Andromeda) by	*Perseus*
	of maiden (Hesione) by	*Hercules*
Rings	twelve hundred, on household table of	*Odysseus*
River	running through stables	*Hercules*
Rock	with woman standing on it	*Theseus*
	lifted by boy, to reveal sword and sandals	*Theseus*
Rocks	Scylla and Charybdis	*Odysseus*
Rose	held by	*Aphrodite*

S

Sabine women	rape of	*Romulus and Remus*
Sacrifice	of cattle flesh to Zeus	*Hermes*
Sandal	one only, being worn by man	*Jason*
Sandals	with sword, under rock	*Theseus*
Scale	held by woman (Justice)	*Seven Virtues*
Scarf	man swimming, with only a scarf about him	*Odysseus*
	being thrown into sea by naked man	*Odysseus*
Sceptre	surmounted by eagle, sacred to	*Zeus*
	surmounted by cuckoo, sacred to	*Hera*
Scorpion	stings man on heel (Orion)	*Artemis*
Sculptor	carving statue of maiden	*Pygmalion*
Sea	chariots surrounded by dolphins	*Poseidon*

Serpent	sacred to	*Apollo*
	being killed by	*Hercules*
	being killed by	*Jason*
	being killed by	*Perseus*
	being killed by	*Apollo*
	being killed by	*Bellerophon*
	Python being killed by	*Artemis and Apollo*
Shepherd	with three maidens	*Judgement of Paris*
	with maidens	*Apulian Shepherd*
Shepherd's crook	sacred to	*Apollo*
Shield	bearing Gorgon Medusa's head in centre, sacred to	*Athena*
	with mirror effect, held by man wearing winged sandals	*Perseus*
Ship	with Golden Fleece on mast	*Jason*
	Argo being built	*Jason*
	with black sail	*Theseus*
Ship's mast	man tied to mast	*Odysseus*
Shooting arrow	at bear	*Callisto and Arcas*
Shower of gold	maiden in tower	*Danae and Zeus*
Sickle	in woman's hand	*Demeter*
Sirens	maidens of the rocks	*Odysseus*
Sleeping man	being taken ashore	*Odysseus*
Snake	biting Eurydice	*Orpheus*
	held by woman (Prudence)	*Seven Virtues*
	man kills one	*Teiresias*
	woman kills one	*Teiresias*
	with nine heads (Hydra)	*Hercules*
Snakes	two being held/killed by child	*Hercules*
	bridal chamber full of snakes (Admetus)	*Artemis*
	growing like hair from woman's head (Medusa)	*Perseus*
Sow	being killed	*Theseus*
Sparrow	heralds spring: sacred to	*Aphrodite*
Spear and helmet	sacred to	*Ares*
Sphinx	man confronted by Sphinx	*Oedipus*
Spring	gushing forth from rock	*Poseidon*
Spying	giant (Polyphemus) spying on lovers	*Acis and Galatea*
Stabbed	man and woman	*Pyramus and Thisbe*
Stabbing	herself on funeral pyre (Dido)	*Dido*
Staff	with pine cone on top	*Dionysus*
Staff of a shepherd	being held by Thalia	*Muse*
Stag	man changing into stag	*Actaeon*
	with golden antlers and brazen hooves	*Hercules*
Stars	which surmount head	*Artemis*
Statue	being admired or held	*Pygmalion*
Stones	falling from sky	*Hercules*
Striking a rock	and salt water gushes forth	*(Athene and Poseidon)*

Stylus	held by Calliope	*The Muse*
Suckled	by a bear	*Atalanta*
	by a she-wolf	*Romulus and Remus*
Swallow	heralds spring	*Aphrodite*
Swan	sacred to	*Apollo*
	large white (Zeus)	*Leda and Zeus*
Swimmer	pierced by arrow (Orion)	*Artemis*
	lies dead on beach, by tower	*Hero and Leander*
Swine	men, under Circe's spell	*Odysseus*
Sword	held by woman (Justice)	*Seven Virtues*
	under rock, with sandals	*Theseus*
T		
Tablets	held by Calliope	*The Muse*
Tamerisk tree	sacred to	*Apollo*
Tapestry	of Penelope	*Odysseus*
	of Arachne	*Arachne*
Tearing men		
asunder	with pine trees (Sinis)	*Theseus*
Three	maidens	*The Graces*
	goddesses, conducted by Hermes	*Hermes*
	witches with man	*Perseus*
	maidens	*Fates*
	maidens (Nemesis)	*Graeae*
	maidens	*Horae*
Three-headed		
dog	Cerberus	*Eros and Psyche*
Throne	sacred to	*Zeus*
Thunderbolt	sacred to	*Zeus*
Torch	burning at night	*Selene*
	in hand	*Eos*
Tower	woman holding lamp, by	*Hero and Leander*
	woman locked in	*Danae and Zeus*
Trident	sacred to	*Poseidon*
Trumpet	heroic trumpet held by woman (Clio)	*The Muse*
Trunk	containing woman and child, on high seas	*Perseus*
Tunic	short, not below knee, worn by	*Artemis*
Turtle	sign of domestic love	*Aphrodite*
	man being thrown to (Scirion)	*Theseus*
Two women	in orchard or garden	*Pomona and Vertumnus*
U		
Urn	woman tilting large urn	*Eos*
	man tilting large urn	*Oceanus*
V		
Vases	woman holding two (Temperance)	*Seven Virtues*
Veil	in wide crescent	*Selene*
	besmirched with blood and lioness	*Pyramus and Thisbe*
Vine leaves	on man's body	*Hercules*
	on man's body	*Odysseus*
Vulture	sacred to	*Apollo*
	perched by man who is chained to a rock	*Prometheus*

W

Walking	on water, Euphemus	*Poseidon*
Wall	between two lovers	*Pyramus and Thisbe*
Warrior	being nursed by maiden, Calypso	*Odysseus*
	prominent in battle	*Hector*
Warrior's body	being tied to chariot	*Hector*
Weaving	tapestry of Penelope	*Odysseus*
	tapestry of Arachne	*Arachne*
Web	of Penelope	*Odysseus*
	of Arachne	*Arachne*
Wheat	in woman's hair	*Demeter*
Wheel	man chained to wheel	*Ixion*
Wheel of fire	and man chained to it	*Ixion*
Whirl-pool	man hanging on tree above	*Odysseus*
Wine	spilt on floor	*Theseus*
Winged boy	Eros	*Eros*
Winged helmet	worn by	*Hermes*
Winged horse	Pegasus	*Bellerophon*
	man mounted on	*Bellerophon*
	ridden by women	*Eos*
Winged man	flying, or dead on rocks	*Icarus*
	flying	*Daedalus*
Winged sandals	worn by	*Hermes*
	worn by	*Perseus*
Winged staff	with serpents (Caduceus)	*Hermes*
Witches	three Graeae (with a man)	*Perseus*
Wolf	sacred to	*Apollo*
	suckling two babies	*Romulus and Remus*
Woman	carrying man away (Orion or Cephalus)	*Eos*
	on rock, awaiting her fate	*Psyche*
	asleep with box at her side	*Psyche*
	carried from burning Troy	*Helen of Troy*
	carried from burning Troy	*Cassandra*
	surrounded by flames (Creusa)	*Jason*
	slain by javelin, man lying across her	*Procris and Cephalus*
	holding lamp above man	*Eros and Psyche*
	leaving ship, with treasures of Troy	*Helen and Menelaus*
	cutting up boy	*Medea*
	shooting arrow at boar	*Meleager and Atalanta*
	stabs herself beside her dead lover	*Pyramus and Thisbe*
	consumed by flames	*Semele and Zeus*
Women, two	in orchard	*Pomona and Vertumnus*
Wooden Horse	at Troy	*Odysseus*
Wreaths	worn by man	*Hercules*
Wrestling	Achelous with two men	*Hercules*
	King Cerycon with two men	*Theseus*
	maiden with lion (Cyrene)	*Apollo*
	man with lion (Nemean lion)	*Hercules*
Writing	above door of house	*Diogenes*

Plate 71. 'Feuilles de Choux'. A fine Flemish Tapestry of the 16th Century woven in Engheim. Size 10′ high × 8′ wide

Index